TATTING

TATTING

Cathy Bryant

Photographs by Ian Platt

B.T. BATSFORD LTD · LONDON

This book is dedicated to
Dr Steven L. Bryant

First published 1992
Reprinted 1993

Typeset by Servis Filmsetting Ltd,
Manchester
and printed in Hong Kong

Published by
B.T. Batsford Ltd
4 Fitzhardinge Street
London W1H 0AH

A catalogue record for this book is available
from the British Library

ISBN 0 7134 6554 9

Contents

Acknowledgements

Special thanks go to the following who tested my first manuscript to see if it did indeed teach them to tat: Mary Lou Bryant, Susan Roberts, Linda Horstmann, Maxine Clinton.

Very special thanks to Ian Platt, who produced all the photographs in this book. His professional skill as well as his time and effort were greatly appreciated.

Thank you to Mary Konior, who encouraged me to send the manuscript to a publisher in the first place.

Finally, thank you to all the tatters, and soon-to-be tatters who take the time to read this book and learn to tat. Because of you the art of tatting will never die!

Introduction

No doubt you have heard that the best way to learn any kind of craft is to watch someone doing it. That's great advice for anyone wanting to learn to knit, crochet, or cross-stitch, because for these hobbies it is relatively easy to find a patient teacher nearby. Many communities even have classes and workshops available. But what of the aspiring tatter? Tatting is enjoying a revival of interest, but experienced tatters and tatting classes are still few and far between. Most pattern books have a brief one-page summary of tatting instructions, but it seems the emphasis here is on the 'brief' and not the 'instructions'! Certainly, it seemed to me, they left a lot unsaid, and therefore misunderstood. It wasn't until I joined a class that I really learned to tat, even though I'd spent hours before then trying to decipher printed instructions. However, once learned, tatting was so easy! I wondered how many others had tried to learn to tat on their own but had failed due to insufficient written instructions. This was my inspiration for writing this book.

This book is a complete beginner's course in tatting. It is written for the novice who has never picked up a shuttle in his or her life.

Therefore, both word and diagram instructions are given for all the techniques, making it as simple as possible to follow. Beginners who already know how to make the double stitch but do not know all the subtleties of tatting will also find this book useful. For example, most students know how to make a join but many do not understand the difference between making a join with the anchor thread and making a join with the working thread. This book is also a reference for more experienced tatters. If you are taking up the craft after a lapse of many years you may find that terminology has changed and that pattern instructions are now as likely to be drawn as written! The decorative techniques and the three-dimensional patterns may also be of interest to those who have only done traditional patterns in the past.

Now is an exciting time to be a tatter. The next few years will, I'm sure, see an explosion of new techniques and refreshing ideas. Master the basics now and you'll have all you need to know to make the beautiful traditional patterns, the exciting modern patterns, and even design some patterns yourself! Happy tatting!

1

Equipment

Thread

The first requirement is that the thread be smooth. In tatting, stitches must be able to slide along an anchor thread, much like a bead sliding along a string. If the thread isn't very smooth this will be difficult and may result in the thread unravelling, becoming fuzzy, or even breaking.

The thread must be able to withstand a fair amount of pulling. If it stretches or frays or breaks easily then tatting will be very difficult. Especially for beginners, choosing a non-elastic thread is very important.

When choosing threads look for the word 'mercerized', meaning the thread has been specially treated. This makes the thread extra smooth as well as extra strong.

When choosing a thread other than cotton check that it has a silky, shiny finish rather than a dull finish. This is a good indication that the thread is very smooth.

Tatting cotton is graded from size 10 (quite thick) to size 100 (very thin). The most popular sizes for Christmas ornaments, placemats and coasters are 10 to 30. Collars are most commonly made from sizes 30 to 50. Handkerchief edgings and dainty lace frills are made from the sizes 50 to 100. Most tatting patterns state which size of thread is required for the article to come out

at stated dimensions. Keep in mind that if you decide to use a finer thread for that pattern the article will be smaller; a thicker thread and it will be larger.

It is not recommended that any thread thinner than size 20 be used when learning any of the techniques in this book, for the simple reason that thinner thread makes it much harder to see what you are doing. However, once the basic techniques have been practised a few times, even the beginner can feel confident in using any size thread, right down to the very dainty size 80!

If you look closely at tatting cotton you will notice that it is actually made up of several strands intertwined. This feature is important if you plan to sew in the ends at the completion of a project.

Shuttle

The first thing to understand right from the beginning is that the shuttle does not make the tatting stitch but simply holds the thread while you make the stitches. However, you will quickly realize that tatting with a shuttle is much easier than it would be without one, so what are its special features? First, the shuttle is small and easy to hold between thumb and forefinger or between thumb and middle finger. It is

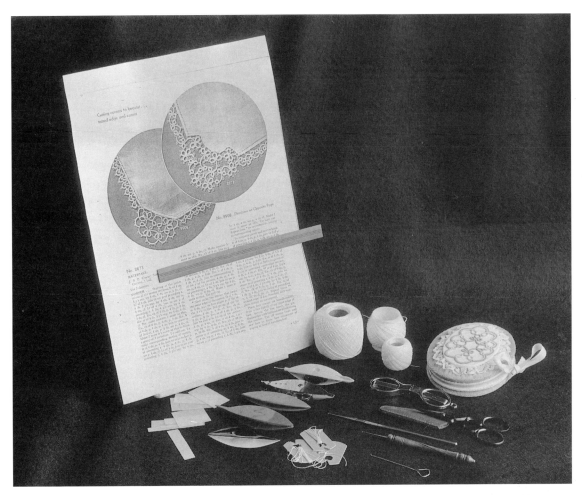

1   Magnetic pattern holder, thread (crochet cotton), needles in case, scissors, fine crochet hooks, thread holders, shuttles and spacers

tapered at the ends to allow it to pass easily between two threads. It also holds a suitable amount of thread and allows easy dispensing of that thread.

There are many kinds of shuttles, but most modern shuttles are made of either metal or plastic and have a removable bobbin. Some may have a hook on one end. If you are lucky enough to own a very old shuttle it is probably made of wood, bone or ivory and has neither a removable bobbin nor a hook. Do not be too concerned about the particular type of shuttle you start with. No doubt, in time you will enjoy collecting and using many types of shuttles.

Scissors

Sharp scissors are essential for making clean cuts in very tight places. Small embroidery scissors do very well, as do the inexpensive folding scissors. The most important requirement for the scissors is that they be easy to handle.

Crochet hook

A small crochet hook is used to make joins. If your shuttle has a hook on one end it can be used instead of a crochet hook, but it is worthwhile to note that the hooks that are built into shuttles are generally quite large and therefore almost certainly not suitable for all your tatting needs.

Needle

A fine needle is needed to neatly sew in the ends of threads after a project is completed. An embroidery needle works very well, or a quilter's needle will do nicely.

Thread holders

After you have been tatting for a while you may find that you have quite a collection of leftover thread. These bits are ideal for practising with, or for making small 'flowers' to glue onto stationery, so do save them! The ideal way to keep these threads neat is to wind them around a holder. My favourite is the plastic bag closure from a loaf of bread, but you can make your own from plastic or card. Write the size of the thread on the holder, because, unless you have an experienced eye, size of thread is difficult to tell by just looking.

Pattern holder

A pattern holder is certainly not an essential item but it might be one of the first extra pieces of equipment you would like to consider buying. Tatting patterns can sometimes be very confusing, with one line looking much like another, especially when you're just glancing at it while tatting. Any type of pattern holder which directs your eye to the current line of instructions could end up being a big timesaver. Presently on the market are metal boards with magnetic strips or magnetic line magnifiers. The pattern is placed on the board with the magnetic strip on top of the pattern at the exact line that you are working. It can save time searching for your place as well as keep you from reading the wrong line.

2

Preparation

Winding a shuttle with removable bobbin

1   Remove the bobbin by holding the shuttle firmly and pushing it out with your thumb. This may be difficult at first but it will become easier as the shuttle is used more.

2   The bobbin may have a small hole on one or both sides. If so, you may tie the end of the thread to the bobbin using this hole [A(i)]. If the bobbin doesn't have a hole, or you do not want to use it, simply tie the thread to the central support of the bobbin [A(ii)].

3   Wind thread onto the bobbin. Do not overfill the bobbin as the extra thread will become tangled.

4   Place the bobbin back in the shuttle. To unwind thread for use, pull the thread with the left hand, holding the shuttle firmly with the right. The bobbin will turn inside the shuttle and allow thread to be dispensed. If too much thread is unwound there is no need to remove the bobbin from the shuttle to rewind the extra thread. Simply turn the bobbin with the thumb and middle fingers of the right hand to rewind the extra thread.

A(i)

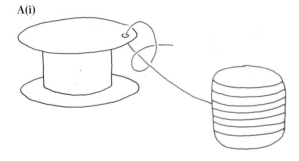

Winding a shuttle with stationary bobbin

1   Secure the thread by tying it to the stationary bobbin within the shuttle [B].

A(ii)

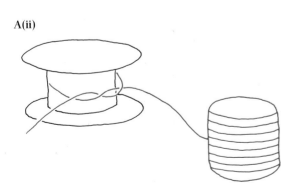

B

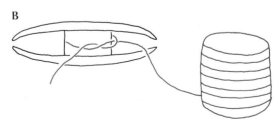

2   Wind the thread onto the bobbin. Do not overfill the bobbin as the extra thread will become tangled.

3   To unwind thread for use, hold the thread with the left hand, and, with the right hand, revolve the shuttle to dispense the thread. If, during use, too much thread is unwound, simply revolve the shuttle so that the extra thread is rewound.

Note: The direction the thread is dispensed from the shuttle is not critical. There are, however, conventions that you should at least be aware of. When working double stitches using method one (see p. 13ff.) the thread should be dispensed from the left, or front, of the shuttle [C]. When using method two (see p. 18ff.) the thread should be dispensed from the right, or back of the shuttle [D]. These conventions allow for the least amount of thread confusion during tatting, although the tatting stitch can be made no matter how the thread comes out of the shuttle.

D

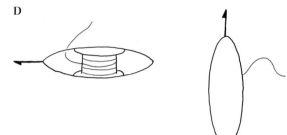

(*left*) side view: hook points towards you, thread unwinds to the back

(*right*) top view: hook points to the left, thread unwinds to the right

C

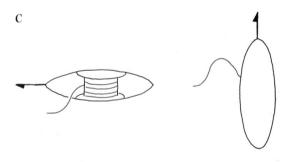

(*left*) side view: hook points towards you, thread unwinds to the front

(*right*) top view: hook points to the left, thread unwinds to the left

Left or right?

Left-handed people may wonder if they should hold the shuttle in the left hand to tat. In actual fact, the conventional method (shuttle in the right hand) also favours left-handed people. While the right hand does little more than hold the shuttle, the left hand actually does most of the thread manipulation work. So if you're left-handed at least try to learn tatting in the conventional way. If it seems too awkward and confusing after several attempts then put the shuttle in the left hand and see if that feels more comfortable. Remember, however, that all instructions in this book are for conventional tatters. So if you want to tat 'left-handed' then you'll have to use mirrors to follow the instructions!

The double stitch: method one

The tatting stitch is called a double stitch simply because it is made in two parts. Each part is called a half stitch. A first half stitch followed by a second half stitch makes up one double stitch. The first time you attempt the double stitch use a thick thread, such as size 10 crochet cotton. In tatting, the right hand does little more than hold the shuttle. Therefore, the diagrams in this section do not show the right hand, only the position of the shuttle.

Preparing threads

1   Wind the shuttle with about 1m (39in) of *light* crochet cotton. Leave a tail of about 25cm (10in) unwound from the shuttle.

2   Knot a length of *dark* coloured crochet cotton to the light thread [A]. The dark coloured cotton may or may not be attached to a whole ball of thread. (Some of the diagrams show a ball attached but you may just have a length of thread.)

3   Hold the knot in the left hand between thumb and forefinger, keeping your other fingers free.

Tension on the ball thread

1   Lay the ball (dark) thread across the back of the fingers of the left hand.

2   Lift the middle fingers slightly and wind the ball thread around the little finger [B].

A

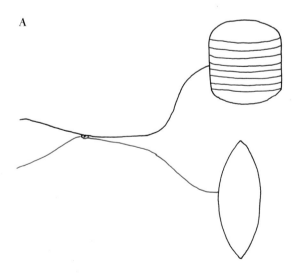

B

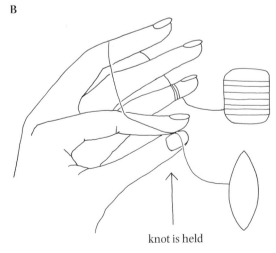

knot is held

3 Press the ring finger and the little finger together so that the ball thread does not loosen and become unwound [C].

C

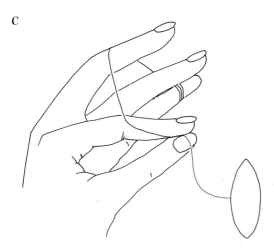

4 Make sure that there is no slack in the ball thread when the middle finger is raised slightly. If there is any slack then the ball thread is not under the correct tension; simply unwind the thread from the little finger and start again.

First half stitch

1 Holding the left hand steady, lay the shuttle (light) thread across the back of the middle finger [D].

D

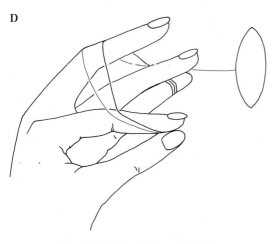

2 Move the shuttle so that it passes from right to left underneath the ball thread [E]. Then bring the shuttle up, between ball and shuttle threads, and take it to the *right* as indicated by the arrow.

E

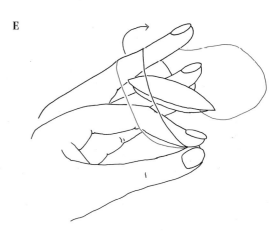

3 Very slowly move the shuttle further to the right. Notice how the shuttle thread pulls on the ball thread [F].

F

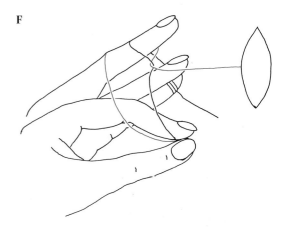

4 Slacken the ball thread by dropping the middle finger. Lower the middle finger away from the ball and shuttle threads, but do not allow the ball thread to come unwound from the little finger. The ball and shuttle threads will then be free [G].

G

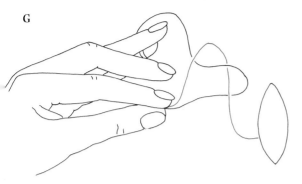

5 Carefully move the shuttle further to the right. Two things will happen. First, the shuttle thread will begin to straighten [H(i)]. Then, as the shuttle thread is pulled taut, the ball thread will appear to 'flip over' the shuttle thread [H(ii)]. Some tatters refer to this action as 'reversing' or 'transferring' the stitch since the shuttle thread starts out being looped around the ball thread and then after the flip the reverse is true – the ball thread is looped around the shuttle thread. The loop has been transferred from shuttle to ball thread. No matter what you decide to call it, make sure you understand the difference between diagrams H(i) and H(ii), that is, before and after the transfer. This is the most critical step in making the basic tatting stitch. It really is the key to

H(i)

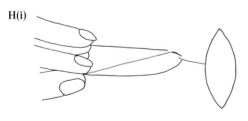

H(ii)

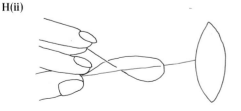

making stitches rather than knots! In fact, having done the transfer, the first half of the double stitch is nearly complete. All that is left to do is tighten up the stitch and position it properly.

6 Raise the middle finger so that it lifts the ball thread. This will cause the stitch to tighten as it slides along the shuttle thread [I].

I

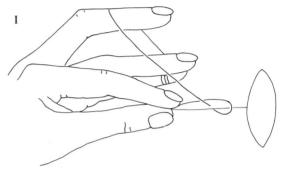

7 Keep tightening the stitch by lifting the middle finger until the stitch is close to the knot held by the thumb and forefinger [J(i)]. The first half of the double stitch is now complete [J(ii)].

J(i)

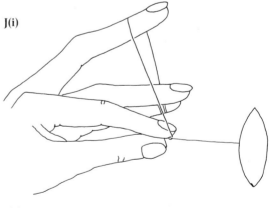

J(ii)

close-up of first half stitch

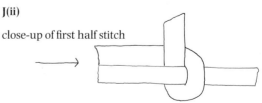

Second half stitch

1   Locate the part of the ball thread that is between the middle and ring fingers. Move the shuttle so that it is behind this thread. Now move the shuttle underneath the middle finger and off to the right [K]. This causes the shuttle thread to go around the ball thread.

K

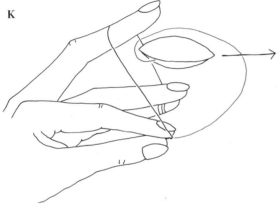

2   Continue moving the shuttle to the right until the shuttle thread is nearly straight [L].

L

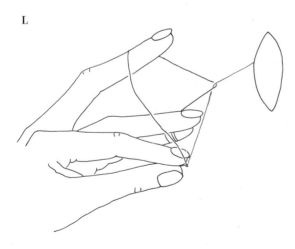

3   Drop the middle finger so that the ball thread is free. Pull the shuttle to the right so that the shuttle thread is completely straight [M].

M

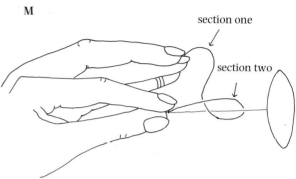

section one

section two

At this point it may be clearer if you think of the ball thread as being in two sections: one section goes from the little finger and loops *under* the shuttle thread; the second section goes from the thumb and loops *over* the shuttle thread. It is the first section that is now important. Locate section one [M].

4   Using the middle finger, lift section one of the ball thread [N]. The loop around the shuttle thread will begin to tighten. The second half of the double stitch is nearly complete.

N

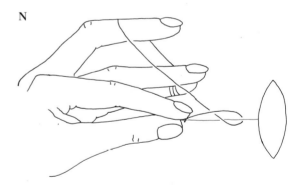

5   Keep raising the middle finger, lifting the ball thread. This will cause the stitch to tighten and slide along the shuttle thread just like the first half stitch did earlier. Keep tightening the stitch until it has positioned itself right next to the first half stitch [O(i)]. The double stitch is now complete [O(ii)].

O(i)

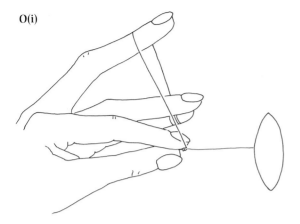

O(ii)
close-up of completed double stitch

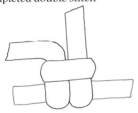

To check that the double stitch has been made correctly hold it between thumb and forefinger and gently slide it along the shuttle thread. If the stitch does not slide then either it has been made incorrectly (a knot) or it is too tight.

If you keep making knots rather than stitches it is probably because one of the half stitches is being made with the wrong thread. In each half of the double stitch make sure it is the ball thread that is making the stitch around the shuttle thread. If this is confusing then go back through each of the diagrams and check which is the ball and

which is the shuttle thread. In particular, practise the transfer of the first half stitch, as shown in diagrams H(i) and H(ii).

Many people do the stitch perfectly but have difficulty sliding it along the shuttle thread. If this happens try to make the stitches looser. Also, stitches may not slide if they are damp from hand perspiration. So if you've had a particularly exasperating lesson then it may be best to put it down for a while and cool off!

Congratulations! You have learned to make double stitches using method one. The next section shows how to tat using method two, but it's important to know beforehand that the resulting double stitches, whether made by method one or method two, will look the same. So if you're just getting used to the first method and don't want to confuse yourself with a new method then it is advisable to miss the next section. You can always go back and learn method two another time.

Naming of threads

It is the ball thread that forms the stitch, and it is the shuttle thread around which the stitch tightens. For this reason the ball thread is often called the *working* thread and the shuttle thread is called the *anchor* thread.

4

The double stitch: method two

Regardless of the method used, the resulting double stitches all look the same. In other words, once a stitch is made it is impossible to tell which method was used. Before learning method two make sure you are familiar with method one. In particular, make sure you understand the terms 'working thread' and 'anchor thread'. For method two it is better if the thread is dispensed from the back of the shuttle, as described in the preparation (see p. 12).

First half stitch

1 Secure the ball (dark) thread by laying it across the back of the fingers of the left hand and winding it around the little finger. Place the ring finger down on the little finger so that the thread does not loosen and become unwound. The ball thread should now be under the correct tension, with no slack [A].

2 Hold the shuttle horizontally between thumb and index finger of the right hand. Raise the shuttle (light) thread with the middle finger so that it is lifted well above the shuttle [A].

3 Keeping all threads taut, pass the shuttle *under* the ball thread [B]. You will feel the ball thread slide between the shuttle and your index finger but your index finger should never completely lose contact with the shuttle.

4 Once the shuttle has passed under the ball thread, it is ready to be drawn back to the original position, this time passing *over* the ball thread [C]. You will feel the ball thread slide between the shuttle and your thumb but your thumb should never completely lose contact with the shuttle. Note that the shuttle is never turned or

A

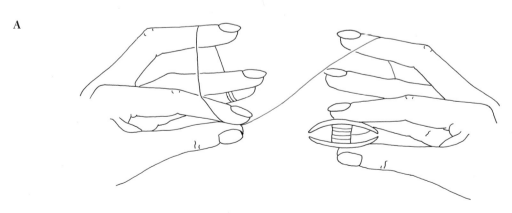

B

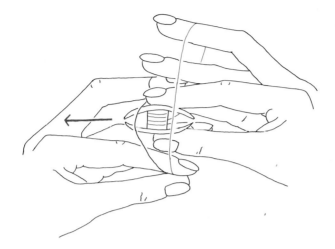

C

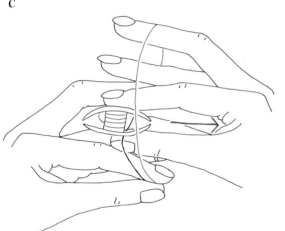

rotated. It 'points' in the same direction throughout the entire manœuvre.

5 Drop the shuttle thread from the middle finger of the right hand and allow the working thread to slacken. Notice at this point how it is the shuttle thread that is looped around the working thread [D].

6 The first half of the double stitch is now ready to be completed in exactly the same manner as for method one. That is, pull the shuttle thread taut so that the working thread 'flips over'. Remember, this is the critical step in which the half stitch is transferred (reversed).

D

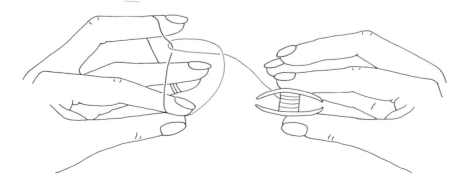

7   Finally, lift the working thread with the middle finger of the left hand, tightening and positioning the first half of the double stitch [E]. This completes the first half of the double stitch.

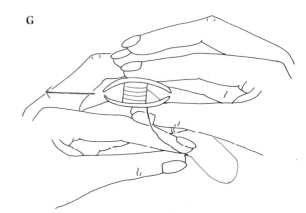

G

E

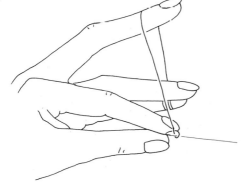

3   The shuttle is now ready to be drawn back to the original position, this time passing *under* the ball thread. The ball thread will slide between the shuttle and index finger [H]. Make sure the loose shuttle thread hangs below the shuttle throughout the entire movement.

H

Second half stitch

1   Hold the shuttle horizontally between thumb and index finger of the right hand. The shuttle thread will hang loose below the shuttle [F].

2   Pass the shuttle *over* the ball thread, allowing the ball thread to slide between the shuttle and the thumb [G].

F

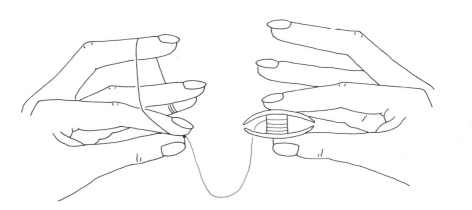

4 At this point, notice how it is the shuttle thread that is making a loop around the taut ball thread [I].

5 Continue pulling the shuttle till the shuttle thread is straight. It will be necessary to slacken the ball thread by dropping the middle finger of the left hand slightly but do not let the ball thread drop off the left hand completely. Pulling the shuttle thread taut causes the ball thread to 'flip over'. As a result of this transfer (reverse), the ball thread will make a loop around the taut shuttle thread. See diagram J (after transfer) and compare it to diagram I (before transfer).

6 Finally, lift the ball thread with the middle finger of the left hand to tighten and position the second half of the double stitch. The double stitch is now complete and should look exactly like a stitch made by method one.

Comparing the two methods

◆ The main difference between method one and method two is how the shuttle is held. For method one the shuttle is held vertically with the thread unwinding from the front. For method two the shuttle is held horizontally with the thread unwinding from the back.

I

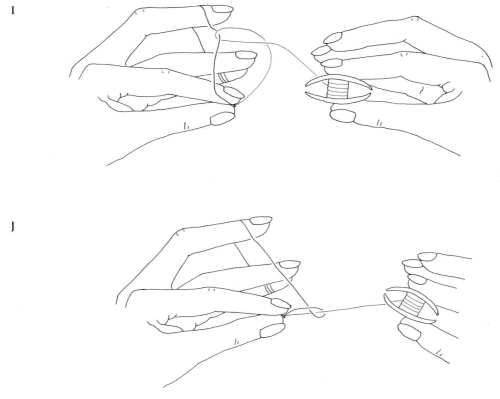

J

◆   Another major difference is how the shuttle thread is manœuvered. For method one the shuttle thread is *looped around* the ball thread. In method two the shuttle thread is passed *under and over* the ball thread with horizontal movements of the shuttle.

◆   Method two is theoretically quicker since the shuttle is held continuously between the thumb and index finger of the right hand. (In method one the right hand switches between middle and index fingers to hold the shuttle.)

◆   Method one requires less thread to be unwound from the shuttle. This can be an advantage when the shuttle is nearly empty!

◆   In practice you will probably discover that one method twists the thread more than the other. Once the thread is twisted it is difficult to tat. So while tatting, take frequent breaks to let the shuttle hang freely, allowing the thread to untwist.

5

Chains

The distinguishing feature of a tatted chain is that it is made using both a ball and a shuttle thread. In fact, if you have learned how to make the double stitch using either method one or two, then you have already made a tatted chain. Diagram A is a close-up of a tatted chain made with a dark coloured ball thread and a light coloured shuttle thread. The arrow shows the direction in which the stitches were made; that is, it points *from the first* stitch *to the last* stitch.

A

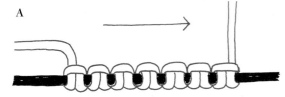

Make sure you know where the thread ends are going in diagram A. On the left, both threads go to a knot held between thumb and forefinger of the left hand. On the right, the dark thread goes to the ball and the light thread goes to the shuttle. If you have trouble understanding where the thread ends go then review the previous sections on the double stitch.

In method one of the double stitch the instructions call for a knot to be made at the very beginning. Many tatting patterns will also begin by having the ball and shuttle

threads 'tied together'. This knot serves as something to hold on to while the first stitch is made. However, once the double stitch is mastered there is no need for this knot to be made at the start. Simply grasp the ball and shuttle threads between thumb and forefinger in the place where the knot would occur, and immediately proceed to make double stitches. At this point don't worry about the chain coming undone because there is no knot. Later, instructions are given for taking care of thread ends in such a way that the tatting will be secure.

To practise making chains, wind some size 10 crochet cotton onto your shuttle and make chains of varying lengths. To vary the length of a chain simply vary the number of double stitches in that chain.

After a chain is made notice that the stitches can slide along the shuttle thread. In fact, they can be purposely slid closer together in order to make the chain 'tighter'. Do not slide stitches so close together that the chain curves excessively.

Rings

The distinguishing feature of a tatted ring is that it is made using *shuttle thread only*. If you have been practising making double stitches with ball and shuttle threads then you will have no trouble learning to make rings.

1   To begin, wind some size 10 crochet cotton onto the shuttle. A full shuttle is not necessary.

2   Grasp the thread in your left hand about 10cm (4in) from the cut end. Hold it between thumb and forefinger [B].

B

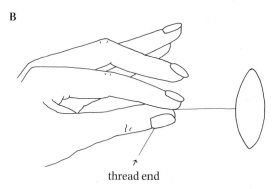

thread end

3   Allow about 33cm (13in) of shuttle thread to show. Lay the thread across the back of the fingers of the left hand, raising the middle fingers slightly [C].

C

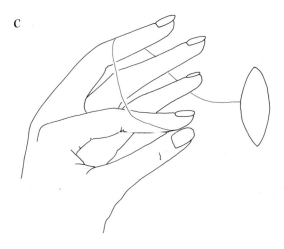

4   Bring the thread forward so that it can once again be caught between thumb and

forefinger of the left hand. Notice how this makes a continuous loop of shuttle thread around the left hand [D].

5   Diagram D should look somewhat familiar to you. Part of the thread lies across the back of the fingers of the left hand and is the working thread section. Part of the thread extends from the thumb and forefinger of the left hand to the shuttle and is the anchor thread section. Make sure that you understand from diagram D how the shuttle thread is both working and anchor threads.

D

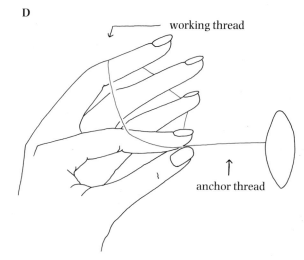

working thread

anchor thread

Which one is working?

When making chains, the working thread is the ball thread and is secured by wrapping around the little finger. When making rings, the working thread is the shuttle thread and is secured by holding between thumb and forefinger. The anchor thread, in both rings and chains, is the shuttle thread.

6 Proceed normally to make a double stitch by either method one or method two. If you refer back to the double stitch sections then substitute the words 'working thread' for 'ball thread' and 'anchor thread' for 'shuttle thread', and remember, to make a ring the working thread is secured between thumb and forefinger, not wrapped around the little finger as for chains.

7 As more stitches are made, the working thread will be used up and you'll notice the left hand being constrained by an ever-tightening loop. To loosen the loop and provide more thread to work with, grasp the thread immediately to the left of the completed stitches and pull [E]. Extra thread

from the shuttle will be pulled through all the stitches, enlarging the working-thread loop. Afterwards, replace the working thread on the left hand correctly and continue making double stitches.

8 As more and more stitches are added, the left hand will automatically grasp the completed stitches in order to make it easier to manœuvre the working thread with the left hand. After the required number of stitches has been completed the ring is ready to be closed [F].

F

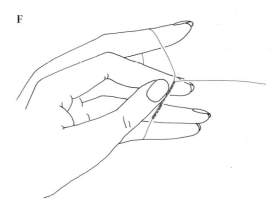

E

9 To close a ring, first release the ring from around the left hand. Grasp the stitches between the thumb and forefinger of the left hand, and grasp the shuttle thread with the right hand [G].

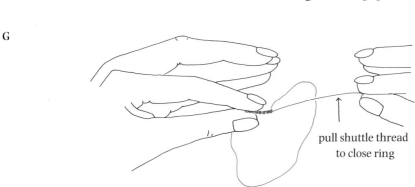

pull this thread to enlarge
working-thread loop

G

pull shuttle thread
to close ring

10 Slowly pull the *shuttle thread* to the right. This will cause the stitches to form a ring and is called 'closing the ring'. When the ring is closed the first stitch will lie next to the last stitch and this juncture is called the 'base of the ring' [H].

H

completed ring

pull shuttle thread in direction of ring to tighten

first stitch

last stitch

shuttle thread

11 Make sure the ring is tightly closed by pulling the shuttle thread firmly in the direction of the ring, as shown in diagram H. Remember, an arrow indicating direction always points from the first stitch and towards the last stitch.

Congratulations! You have made a tatted ring. After making one ring, leave a short length of thread, called a 'space', and proceed to make another ring. Do this several times to end up with a series of rings [I].

Opening a closed ring

There may be times when a ring has been made incorrectly and must be redone. To do this, the ring must be opened and unpicked. This can be a tedious and tricky procedure, especially if the ring is closed very tightly or is made with very fine thread, but it is not impossible.

1 Separate two stitches enough to enable a small crochet hook to catch the anchor thread between them [J].

J

I first ring made

last ring made

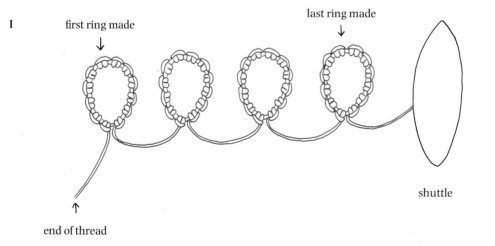

shuttle

end of thread

2 Using a fine crochet hook pull the anchor thread in an anticlockwise direction. This should allow the shuttle thread to be pulled through the last stitches, therefore opening the ring [K].

K

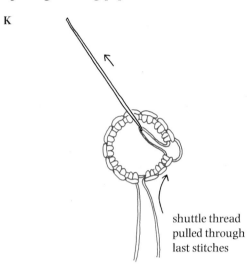

shuttle thread pulled through last stitches

3 When a significant amount of shuttle thread has been pulled through the last stitches then all the stitches can be slid back together. The gap will then be at the base of the ring and will look more like an unclosed ring [L].

L

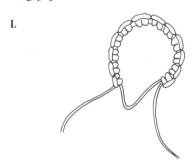

4 At this point the loop should be fairly easy to enlarge even further. When the loop is large enough the ring should look exactly as it did before it was ever closed. Stitches can then be added or unpicked or the whole ring can be unpicked.

Reversing the work

Many tatting patterns begin with a ring followed by a chain, then proceed with alternating rings and chains. This may sound confusing at first but it's really very easy. It does require a new technique called 'reversing the work'.

1 Wind the shuttle about half full of size 10 crochet cotton. Do not cut this thread from the ball. Hold the shuttle in your right hand as usual and allow the ball to rest in your lap.

2 Grasp the thread anywhere with your left hand and proceed to make a fairly large ring, say of 15 to 20 double stitches. Make sure you close the ring tightly.

3 Look at the ring you've just made. Notice that the thread going off to the right is attached to the shuttle, and the thread going off to the left is attached to the ball [M].

M   before reversing the work

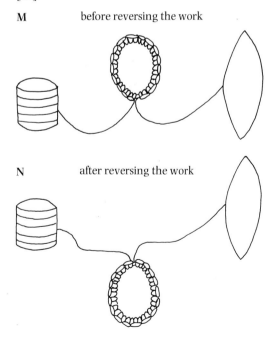

N   after reversing the work

4 Flip the ring so that it is upside-down and the threads are at the top [N]. This simple action is called 'reversing the work', or simply 'turning'.

5 The ball, ring, and shuttle are now in position to make a chain. Hold the ring between thumb and forefinger of the left hand; wrap the ball thread around the little finger so that it is in the correct position and under the correct tension, and then proceed to make a chain of, say, 10 to 15 double stitches.

6 After finishing the chain, reverse the work again, so that the ring is once again 'upright'. The work is now in position to make another ring. Diagrams O and P show the work before and after this second reversing the work.

7 Continue making alternating rings and chains. Diagram Q shows the work after four rings and three chains have been completed. Notice how the work proceeds from left to right, with the rings and chains numbered according to the order in which they were made.

O

before reversing the work

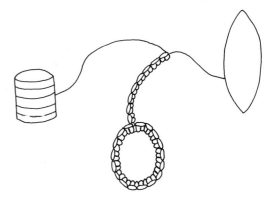

P

after reversing the work

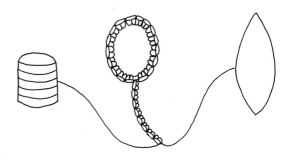

Q

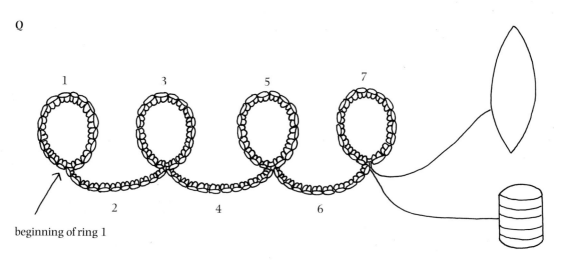

beginning of ring 1

Tips

◆ Remember to reverse the work each time a ring or chain is completed.

◆ Make sure that the first stitch of a new ring or chain is right next to the last stitch of the previous ring or chain. This will make the tatting look continuous and neat.

◆ To make the transition from ring to chain even more smooth, try starting the chain with a second half stitch. This half stitch won't count as a whole stitch and only serves to fill the tiny gap that normally appears when changing from ring to chain. After making the half stitch proceed normally with complete double stitches. Try changing from ring to chain both with and without this half stitch to see if you can tell the difference. If you like the difference then it will become second nature to you to include it every time you go from a ring to a chain, even though no pattern will ever call for it explicitly.

Cutting out a ring

There is bound to come a time when you'll be tatting along, happily making rings and chains, and then you'll realize that there is a mistake in one of the rings made some time ago. If you can live with the mistake (that is, it doesn't affect the pattern at all), then fine. But if it's a mistake that you can't live with then there is nothing for it but to cut out the offending ring and redo it. The unfortunate catch is that all tatting done after the offending ring will also be cut out.

Cutting out a ring can also be used instead of opening a closed ring and unpicking it. Sometimes, no matter how hard you try, a ring simply will not open, usually because the ring had been closed very tightly and the anchor thread cannot slide through the stitches, or because the thread is very fine and tends to break before you can get the ring opened. As a last resort, the offending ring must be cut out.

1 Separate the first and last stitches by a tiny amount to reveal the anchor thread at the base of the ring [R].

R

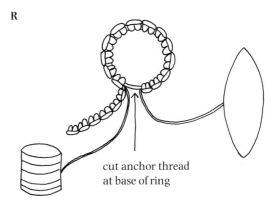

cut anchor thread
at base of ring

2 Using a pair of sharp scissors, cut the anchor thread at the base of the ring. Make sure no other threads are cut!

3 Once the anchor thread is cut all the stitches will unravel and you'll be left with a rather short thread in the place where the ring used to be. It is important to notice that the ball thread is still intact and attached to the tatting [S].

4 A new ring is ready to be made using a new shuttle thread. Later in this book the section on joins will give detailed instructions on how to attach the new shuttle thread to the work already in progress.

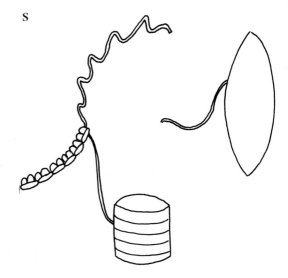

S

6

Picots

In tatting, picots are loops made by the working thread. They can be made simply for decoration or for the purpose of joining.

1   Make two double stitches. (It doesn't matter if you're working on a ring or a chain.)

2   Leave a small space, say 1cm ($\frac{3}{8}$in), on both the working and anchor threads, then make a third double stitch [A].

A

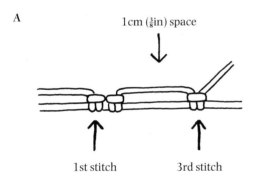

3   Slide the third stitch along the anchor thread so that it is next to the second stitch. The working thread will form a loop between the second and third stitches [B]. This loop is called a picot.

B

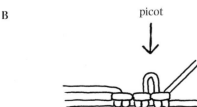

4   Continue making picots. The longer the space between the stitches, the longer the picot [C]. Note that the height of the picot is roughly one half the length of the space that was left to make it. Therefore, a 13mm ($\frac{1}{2}$in) space makes a 6mm ($\frac{1}{4}$in) picot. Finally, notice that if several picots are made consecutively, as in diagram C, there is always one double stitch between the picots.

Patterns may call for one or more stitches between picots. So instructions calling for 'three double stitches, picot, three double stitches, picot, one double stitch', means 'complete three double stitches, leave a space to form the picot, complete three more double stitches, leave another space to form the second picot, complete the final double stitch, then slide all stitches together', and would look like this:

D

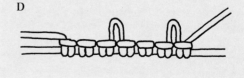

C

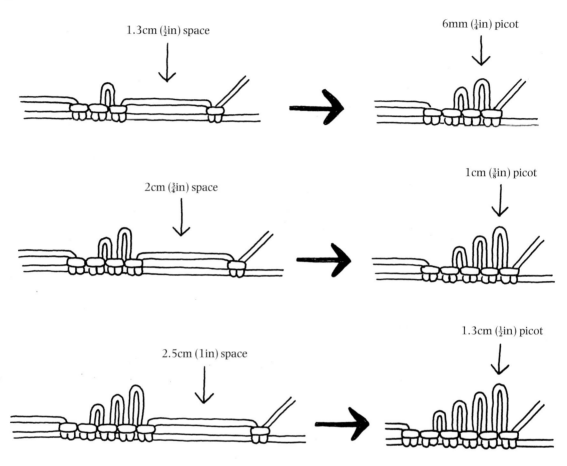

1.3cm (½in) space

6mm (¼in) picot

2cm (¾in) space

1cm (⅜in) picot

2.5cm (1in) space

1.3cm (½in) picot

Practise making picots

Practise making series of picots according to the sets of instructions below. The lengths of the picots may vary, but the number of stitches between picots must follow the instructions. Check your work by looking at the diagrams illustrating each set of instructions. (Note that the diagrams are shown as chains. However, each set of instructions can be worked into a ring if you wish.)

1   Two double stitches, picot, three double stitches, picot, one double stitch, picot, three double stitches, picot, two double stitches

2   Five double stitches, picot, five double stitches, picot, five double stitches, picot, five double stitches

3   Four double stitches, picot, four double stitches, picot, one double stitch, picot, one double stitch, picot, one double stitch, picot, four double stitches, picot, four double stitches

4   One double stitch, picot, one double stitch, picot, one double stitch, picot, six double stitches, picot, one double stitch, picot, one double stitch, picot, one double stitch

E

1

2

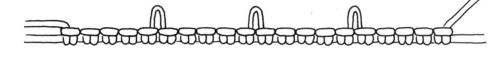

3

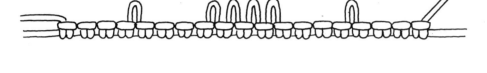

4

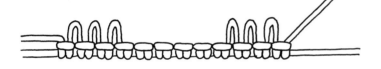

7

Joins

Joining is a technique that allows you to connect your line of rings and chains to make motifs. The connections can be made to join ring to ring, ring to chain, or chain to chain. The two most common places to join are to a picot and to the base of a ring. A join can be made using either the working thread or the anchor thread.

Join to a picot using the working thread

1 Begin by making a ring, a chain, and part of a second ring according to the following instructions:

Ring 1: five double stitches, picot, five double stitches, picot, five double stitches, picot, five double stitches, close ring, reverse work
Chain: three double stitches, picot, three double stitches, picot, three double stitches, reverse work
Ring 2: five double stitches, DO NOT CLOSE THIS RING YET!!!

2 Position ring 1 so that the last picot is very near the last stitch just made on ring 2 [A]. (For clarity, the section of the anchor

A

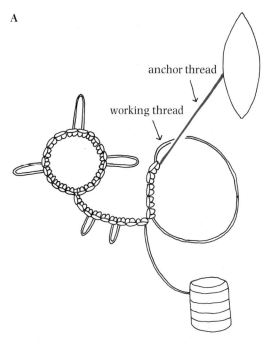

anchor thread

working thread

B

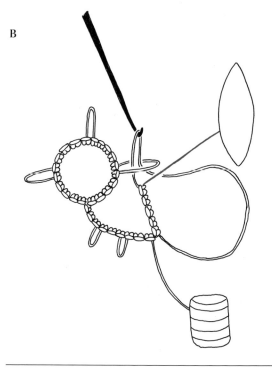

thread from ring 2 to the shuttle is coloured in the diagram.)

Note: You may find it easier to remove ring 2 from around the left hand while you make a join. With practice you'll learn how to make joins with the working thread still around the left hand.

3   With a small crochet hook pull the *working thread* of ring 2 up through the last picot of ring 1 [B].

4   Push the shuttle through the loop formed by the working thread [C].

5   Pull the working thread back down through the picot. Notice that now ring 2 is joined to ring 1 [D].

6   Position the working thread around the left hand and complete ring 2: five double stitches, picot, five double stitches, picot, five double stitches. Make sure that the first double stitch after the join is positioned right next to the join.

D

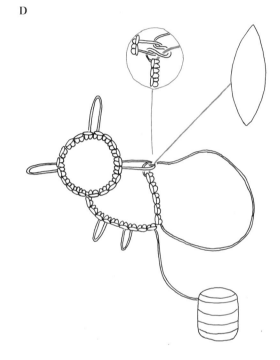

C

7   Before closing ring 2 check that the stitches both before and after the join are able to slide along the anchor thread. If they do not slide then a knot has been made and the stitches must be unpicked and redone. If all is well close the ring as normal [E].

E

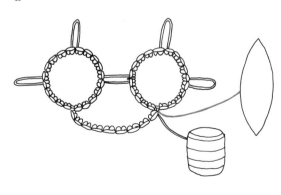

Join to a picot using the anchor thread

1 Begin by making a ring and a chain according to the following instructions:

> *Ring:* five double stitches, picot, five double stitches, picot, five double stitches, picot, five double stitches, close ring, reverse work
>
> *Chain:* nine double stitches, picot, nine double stitches (DO NOT REVERSE WORK)

2 Position the chain so that the last stitch made is very close to the second picot of the ring [F]. Notice how this is done by *rotating* the ring, not reversing it.

F

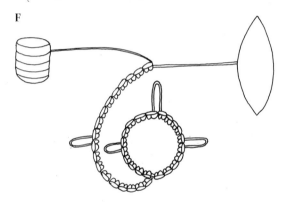

3 With a small crochet hook pull the *anchor thread* up through the second picot of the ring [G].

G

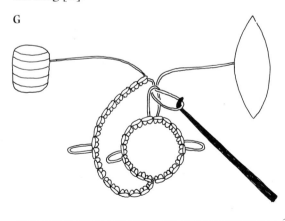

4 Push the shuttle through the loop formed by the anchor thread [H].

H

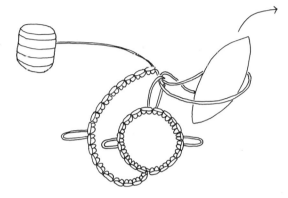

5 Pull the anchor thread so that the join is tightened. Notice that now the chain is joined to the ring [I].

I

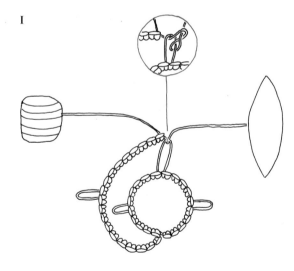

6 Position the working thread on the left hand correctly and complete the chain: nine double stitches, picot, nine double stitches [J].

J

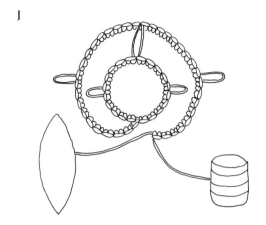

follow are for using the anchor thread but you may want to try it with the working thread to see the difference it makes.

1 Follow steps 1–6 as for 'Join to a picot using the anchor thread'. Position the work so that the last stitch of the chain is near the base of the ring.

2 Look at the base of the ring carefully. Notice that there is a small loop created by the transition from ring to chain. This tiny loop is magnified in the close up view in diagram K.

K

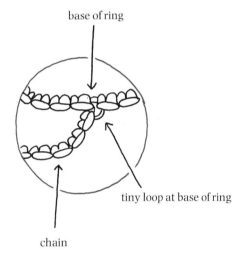

base of ring

tiny loop at base of ring

chain

Anchor thread joins

It is important to note that a join using the anchor thread makes a knot in the work. That is, the stitches before the join can no longer slide along the anchor thread. Therefore, before making a join using the anchor thread make sure that all previous stitches have been slid along the anchor thread to the correct tightness.

Join to the base of a ring

It is very common for a pattern of alternating rings and chains to end by joining the last chain made to the first ring made. Since there is no picot at the beginning of the ring the join must be made to the base of the ring.

Joining to the base of a ring can be done using either the working thread or the anchor thread. The instructions which

Note: There will only be a tiny loop at the base of the ring if the shuttle thread was never cut from the ball thread at the very beginning. So, for example, if you decided to use one colour of thread for the ball thread and another colour of thread on the shuttle, then you will have thread *ends* at the base of the ring and not a tiny loop. In this case, simply tie the thread ends together to join the chain to the base of the ring.

3 Using a small crochet hook pull the anchor thread up through this small loop [L].

L

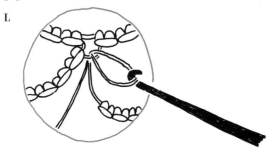

4 Finish the join as normal: push the shuttle through the loop formed by the anchor thread, and then pull the anchor thread to tighten the join [M]. The chain is now joined to the base of the ring.

M

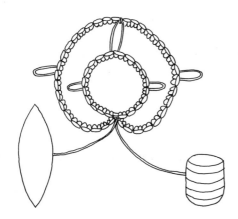

Join within a motif

In many motif patterns a final join is required to 'close' the motif. This join can be difficult to do without twisting the picot, which is untidy. The instructions which follow show how to master this type of join without twisting the picot.

1 Diagram N shows an incomplete pattern:

Ring 1: five double stitches, picot, six double stitches, picot, six double stitches, picot, five double stitches, close
Ring 2: five double stitches, join to the last picot of previous ring, six double stitches, picot, six double stitches, picot, five double stitches, close
Ring 3: as ring 2
Ring 4: as ring 2
Ring 5: five double stitches, join to last picot of ring 4, six double stitches, picot, six double stitches, (leave this ring incomplete at this point).
The fifth ring is ready to be joined to the first picot of the first ring.

N

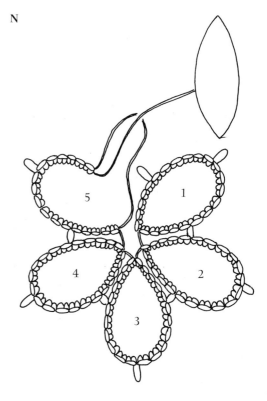

2 To make the join without twisting the picot, begin by folding the motif so that the *back* of ring 1 faces you. The picot to be joined should be prominent [O].

O

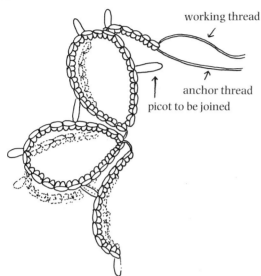

working thread

anchor thread

picot to be joined

3 Now concentrate on the picot that is to be joined. Insert a crochet hook into the picot from the *back* (that is, the hook will point towards you as it is put into the picot) [P].

P

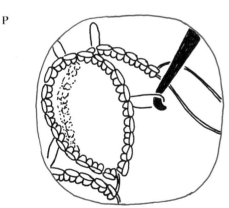

4 Turn the crochet hook so that it points away from you and is in position to catch the working thread of the unfinished ring. At this point the picot will indeed be twisted [Q].

Q

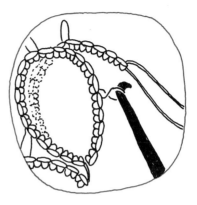

5 Catch the working thread of the unfinished ring with the crochet hook and pull it through the picot [R].

R

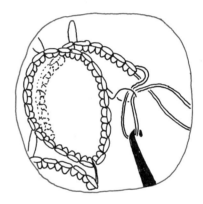

6 Push the shuttle through the loop formed by the working thread [S].

S

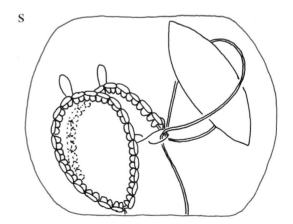

7 Pull the working thread back down through the picot to secure the join. Ring 5 can be finished from this position: complete the last five double stitches.

8 Close Ring 5. The motif will naturally unfold as the ring is closed. Notice how the join between ring 1 and ring 5 is smooth, without twisting the picot [T].

T

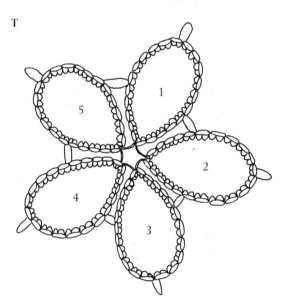

Join into a previously made join

This technique is a special type of join that forms an interesting tatting feature. The following instructions are for joining into a previously made join using the *anchor thread*, but the technique can also be done using the working thread.

1 Begin with an incomplete motif [U]:
Ring: five double stitches, picot, five double stitches, picot, five double stitches, picot, five double stitches, picot, five double stitches, close, reverse work
Chain: six double stitches, join to fourth picot of ring using anchor thread, six double stitches, join to third picot of ring

U

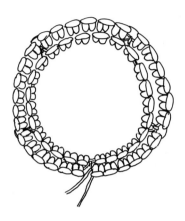

using anchor thread, six double stitches, join to second picot of ring using anchor thread, six double stitches, join to first picot of ring using anchor thread, six double stitches, join to base of ring using anchor thread (DO NOT REVERSE WORK).

2 Continue the chain by adding seven double stitches. The work is now ready to be joined to the previously made join.

3 Carefully look at the first join between the chain and the ring. Notice how there is a tiny gap between the stitch before and the stitch after the join, due to the anchor thread being used for the join. It is into this tiny gap that the current join is going to be made [V].

V

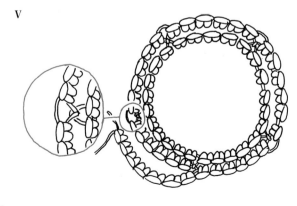

4   Using a small crochet hook pull the anchor thread of the current chain up through the tiny gap between the two stitches on either side of the previously made join [W].

W

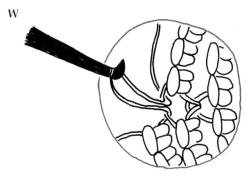

X

5   Finish the join as usual and tighten it securely. You may even find that once the join is made the tiny gap of the previous join is more noticeable.

6   Continue the chain with seven more double stitches, then join to the next previously made join. Repeat this twice more and end by adding seven double

stitches and making a final join. The work should look something like that in diagram [X].

7   You can now continue with several rounds of chains, increasing the number of double stitches between joins on each round. This technique is used to make the small mat in the patterns section. Notice how the little gaps at the joins actually become a feature of the tatting.

8

Tatting with two shuttles

There are two meanings to the phrase 'two shuttle tatting'. In old patterns, two shuttles are called for to make chains (as opposed to requiring just one shuttle to make rings only). In this case, the second shuttle acts exactly like a ball of thread. It is never actually picked up and worked with, but simply used to supply thread as if it were a ball of thread. In modern patterns, two shuttles are needed when they are *both* to be used as working threads.

Preparation

1   First, take two shuttles and mark them so that you know which is shuttle one and which is shuttle two. (A dot of nail varnish or a small sticker on one shuttle works well and can be removed later when you no longer need the markings.)

2   Wind the thread onto shuttle one from a ball of thread as normal, but DO NOT CUT THREAD AWAY FROM THE BALL AFTER FILLING THE SHUTTLE.

3   Unwind a considerable length of thread from the ball and cut. Starting with this cut end, wind the thread onto shuttle two. Both shuttles are now wound with a common thread [A].

Method

1   To begin, treat shuttle two as if it were a ball of thread and use shuttle one to make a ring of 15 double stitches. Reverse the work as normal and proceed to make a chain of 10 double stitches. After making the chain DO NOT REVERSE THE WORK. Your work should look like that in diagram B. Notice that shuttle one holds the anchor thread for the chain and shuttle two holds the working thread.

B

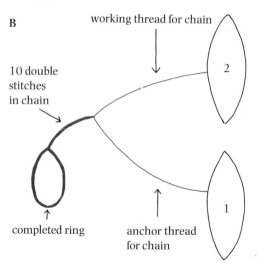

working thread for chain

2

10 double stitches in chain

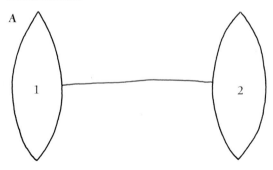

completed ring

anchor thread for chain

1

A

1   2

2   Drop shuttle one and pick up shuttle two. Proceed to make a ring of 10 double stitches with shuttle two. The first stitch of the ring should be made as close as possible to the last stitch of the chain [C]. The arrow in diagram C points in the direction that the ring was made.

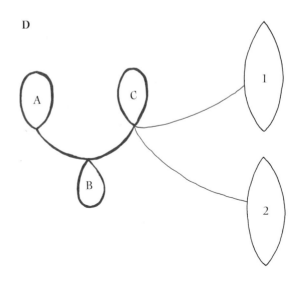

D

C

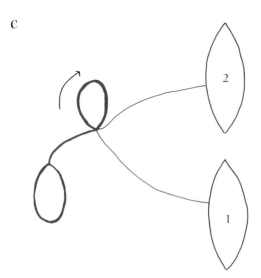

3   Drop shuttle two and pick up shuttle one. Again treat shuttle two as if it were a ball of thread and continue making the chain, adding 10 more double stitches. Reverse the work as usual after the chain is completed, then, with shuttle one, make another ring of 15 double stitches. Diagram D shows the completed work with the rings lettered in the order in which they were made.

Why use two shuttles?

Two shuttle tatting is used whenever you wish to avoid crossing threads. Here is an example to illustrate the technique. Ring B in diagram D could be called a 'ring-on-a-chain' since no reverse work was done either before or after it was made. But you may wonder *why* a second shuttle was required to make it. Let's take a closer look . . .

1   Reverse the work already completed, shown in diagram D, and add another chain of 10 double stitches. (Remember, shuttle two will hold the working thread for this chain.) Now look carefully at the last stitch [E]. Notice how the thread from shuttle two is *above* the thread from shuttle one. (Shuttle one thread is coloured in the diagram for clarity.)

E

shuttle two thread

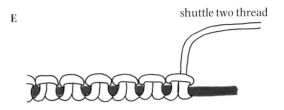

shuttle one thread

2   Try to visualize what would happen if shuttle one were used to make the ring-on-a-chain. To make the very first stitch the thread from shuttle one would have to be *crossed over* the thread from shuttle two [F].

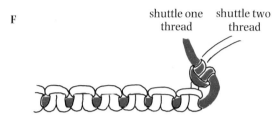

F

shuttle one thread   shuttle two thread

3 In the interest of education, try making a ring-on-a-chain using shuttle one [G]. Notice how the threads are crossed twice: once just before and once just after the ring-on-a-chain. You may notice other things about this ring-on-a-chain. For instance, it may not want to lay flat, or it may want to lean to one side. Also, the transitions from chain to ring will not be smooth. These problems are all due to the threads being crossed.

G

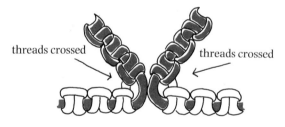

base of a ring-on-a-chain made with shuttle one

threads crossed   threads crossed

4 Now look back at diagram E and visualize what would happen if shuttle two were used to make the ring-on-a-chain. Since the thread from shuttle two is already 'on top', the ring could be made without crossing over the thread from shuttle one. Even after the ring is completed the thread from shuttle two would still be on top, ready to act as the working thread for the

continued chain. No threads would be crossed before or after the ring-on-a-chain. Try making a ring-on-a-chain using shuttle two. When completed it should lay flat and smooth [H].

H

base of a ring-on-a-chain made with shuttle two

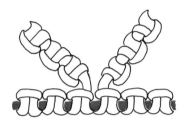

Uses of two shuttle tatting

Most patterns will state at the beginning whether one or two shuttles are needed, but be careful about accepting this information as absolute. As stated earlier, very old patterns may call for two shuttles when one shuttle and one ball is all that's needed. In other patterns shuttle and ball are called for but then the pattern requires that the threads be crossed. In almost all cases of this type the pattern would look much neater if two shuttles were used and the threads not crossed. So before starting a pattern, study it and decide for yourself if two shuttle tatting would be appropriate. With a little experience you will be able to look at any tatting pattern and decide if two shuttles are needed. What follows is a short list of the more common patterns that require two shuttles.

Ring-on-a-chain

In diagram I rings 1, 3, and 5 are made with shuttle one as normal. ('Normal' in this context means doing a reverse work before each ring or chain.) Rings 2 and 4 are each a ring-on-a-chain, made with shuttle two. All chains arc made with shuttle two as the *working* thread.

I

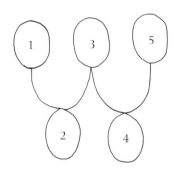

Reverse chain

This example makes it possible for a pattern to change direction. Look at diagram J. All rings are made with shuttle one as normal. All chains are made with shuttle two as the working thread *except the reverse chain*, which is made with shuttle one as the working thread. Note also that no reverse work is done just before or just after the reverse chain.

J

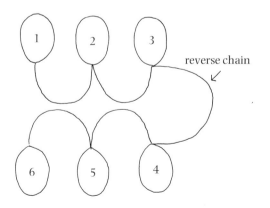

reverse chain

Ring/Ring

This pattern could actually be done with one shuttle and one ball without being too untidy, though strictly speaking it would require threads to be crossed. Try making it first with one shuttle then with two shuttles and make your own comparison. For the two shuttle version see diagram K. Rings 1, 2, 4, 5, and 7 are made with shuttle one. Rings 3 and 6 are made with shuttle two. All chains are made with shuttle two as working thread.

K

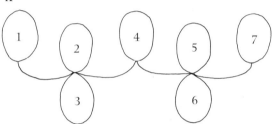

Switching

This last example requires that the shuttles are switched after every ring/chain couple. Study diagram L. The pattern is 'ring, chain; clover, chain; ring, chain; clover, chain . . .' (A clover is simply three rings made consecutively, with no reverse work or chains in between.) Rings 1, 3, and 5 are made with shuttle one. Clovers 2 and 4 are made with shuttle two. A reverse work is

L

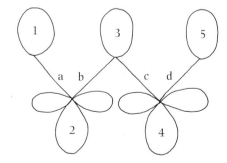

done *before* each ring or clover but *not before the chains*. Chains a and c are made with shuttle one as working thread, but chains b and d are made with shuttle two as working thread. The unique property of this pattern is that it forces the chains to form sharp 'V' shapes, with the rings and clovers at the points of the 'V's. Compare this pattern with the ring-on-a-chain pattern in diagram I. Notice that in the ring-on-a-chain pattern the chains form 'U' shapes, not sharp 'V' shapes.

9

Finishing ends

When a tatting pattern is complete something must be done with the thread ends. This section gives several methods of dealing with thread ends: sewing, glueing, and weaving.

Sewing

This method of finishing off ends is successful for patterns using cotton sized 10 to 40. Each end should be cut so that it is about 10cm (4in) long. If the thread end is shorter then sewing will be difficult.

1   Hold the thread end between thumb and forefinger and roll it so that the three individual strands of the thread become unwound [A].

A

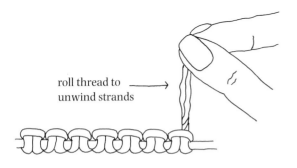

roll thread to unwind strands

2   Separate out one strand completely from the other two [B].

B

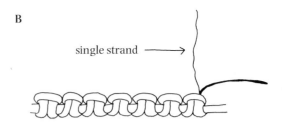

single strand ⟶

3   Lay the two strands along the nearest stitches and thread a fine needle with the separated strand [C].

C

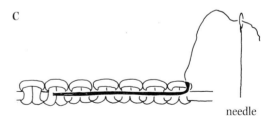

needle

4   Proceed to 'sew' the two strands to the tatting [D]. Make about four or five stitches to tack down the two strands, then oversew two stitches to secure the sewing thread [E].

D   single strand sewn over the two strands

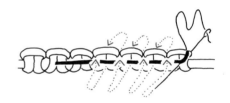

E   oversew to secure sewing thread

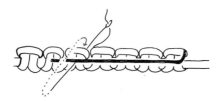

5   Cut the strands close to the tatting.

6   If two thread ends are very close to each other tie them together before proceeding to sew in each end separately [F].

F

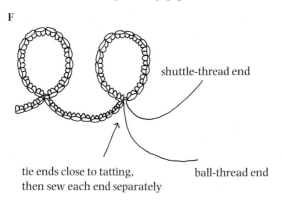

shuttle-thread end

tie ends close to tatting,
then sew each end separately   ball-thread end

Glueing

If a project is made using very fine thread, thinner than size 40, it may be difficult to separate out individual strands for sewing.

To secure these ends it is usually easiest and neatest to simply cut the end to about 6mm ($\frac{1}{4}$in) and then glue this bit right onto the nearest stitches, using a waterproof glue. If two thread ends are close, as in diagram F, tie them together before proceeding to cut and glue each end.

Weaving in to work in progress

Since a shuttle only holds a limited amount of thread there are bound to be times when the shuttle runs out of thread before a

G

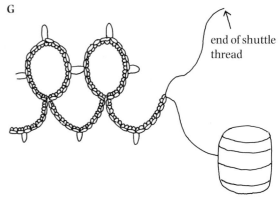

end of shuttle thread

pattern is completed [G]. If possible, try and get to a point in the pattern where a ring is ready to be made. Now join in a new shuttle thread to the work already in progress:

1   Cut the loose shuttle thread to within about 10cm (4in) of the tatting. Refill the shuttle, preferably with thread from a spare ball, *not* from the ball of thread attached to the tatting. If you have to use the ball attached to the tatting, unwind enough thread from the ball to finish the pattern before cutting. Otherwise, you'll have a ball thread end to take care of as well!

2   With the newly filled shuttle, begin the next ring of the pattern. In fact, just make the first half of the first double stitch, and allow it to be very loose so that the loop is still quite visible [H]. (The left hand is not shown in the diagram so that the threads can be seen clearly.)

H

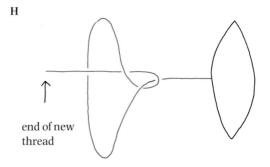

end of new thread

3 Pick up the tatting already in progress and slip the old thread end through the loop made by the first half of the new double stitch [I]. Tighten the first half of the double stitch and slide it along the old thread end so that it is positioned right next to the last stitches made. Note how the old thread end acts like an *anchor* thread, not a working thread.

I

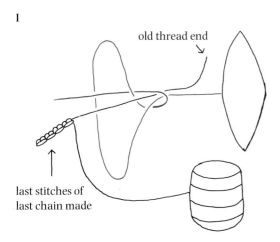

old thread end

last stitches of
last chain made

4 Make the second half of the double stitch, again leaving it very loose. Slip the old thread end through this loop before tightening the stitch [J]. Continue making

J

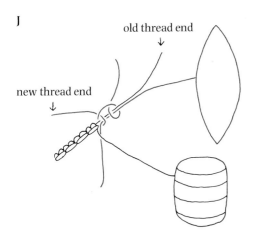

old thread end

new thread end

double stitches, slipping the old thread end through each half stitch loop before tightening. This is called 'weaving in the end'.

5 After the old thread end has been woven into five stitches or so, it can be dropped. Finish the ring as normal and close it. The old thread end will stick out of the tatting [K].

K

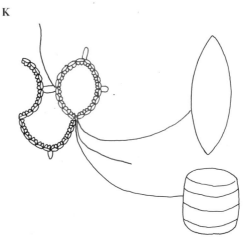

6 Now it's the turn of the new thread end (the thread end from the newly refilled shuttle.) First, cut the end to within 10cm (4in) of the tatting and position the work so that it is ready to make the next chain (or ring) of the pattern. Make the first half stitch as before, leaving it very loose. Slip the thread end through the loop of the half stitch and tighten. Continue in this way for several stitches. Make sure that the thread end acts as an *anchor* thread, not a working thread, regardless of whether a chain or a ring is being made. After weaving the thread end into four or five double stitches, drop it and finish the chain (or ring) as normal.

7   Now that both the old and the new thread ends have been woven into the work they can be cut close to the tatting, giving a neat and tidy look [L].

L

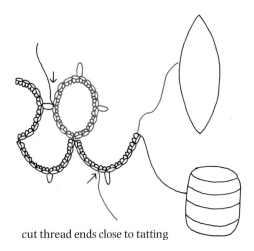

cut thread ends close to tatting

One last note about weaving in the ends. If a pattern is started with a shuttle thread *not* attached to a ball thread (for example, maybe the shuttle thread is a different colour to the ball thread) then weaving in the ends can be used at the *beginning* of this piece of work to get rid of the ends (instead

M

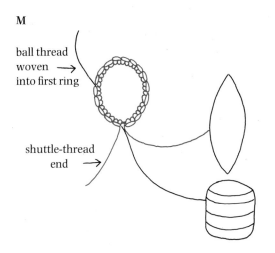

ball thread woven ⟶ into first ring

shuttle-thread end ⟶

of sewing them in later on). As the first ring of the pattern is made weave in the ball thread end [M]. Then, as the first chain of the pattern is made weave in the shuttle thread end [N].

N

shuttle thread woven into first chain

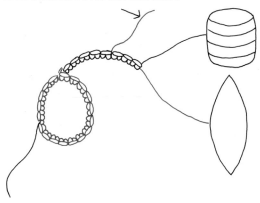

Weaving in final ends

This technique is similar to the technique of joining to work in progress, so if you have practised that technique then weaving in final ends will not be difficult to learn.

1   Many patterns end with a final chain followed by a final ring [O]. Since there will

O

final ring

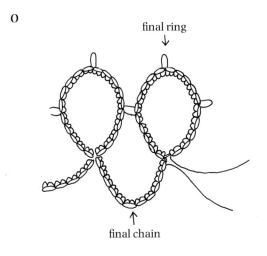

final chain

be two thread ends to deal with (a ball thread end and a shuttle thread end) both the final chain and the final ring will be used.

2   Let's say the final chain is to have 10 double stitches. Make five of those double stitches (with picots if called for) and then pause. Pick up a 20cm (8in) length of thread and fold it in half. Ideally this separate piece of thread should be *thinner* than the thread being tatted. So if size 40 thread is being tatted then a size 60 or 80 would be suitable. This separate length of thread is going to be woven into the last five stitches of the final chain. Make a loose half stitch and slip the folded length of thread through the loop, *folded end first* [P]. Tighten the half stitch and position it properly in the chain.

P

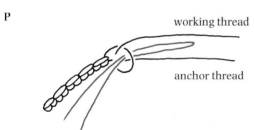

working thread

anchor thread

3   Make the second half of the double stitch, again leaving it very loose. Slip the folded thread through the loop then tighten and position the stitch [Q]. Make sure that the folded thread acts as an *anchor* thread.

Q

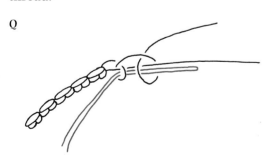

4   Finish the final chain, weaving the folded thread through each half stitch. When the chain is complete the folded thread will extend beyond the end of the chain, forming a loop [R]. Now the final ring is ready to be made.

R

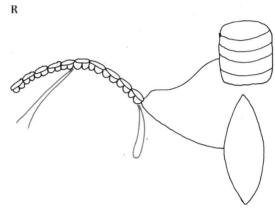

folded thread woven into final chain

5   Make the final ring as normal until the last four or five stitches. Pick up another 20cm (8in) piece of thin thread, fold in half, and proceed to weave it into the last stitches of the ring, as with the chain [S].

S

6 When the final ring is completed and closed the folded piece of thread will extend out of the base of the ring, forming a loop [T].

T

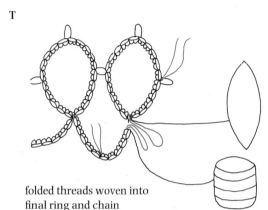

folded threads woven into final ring and chain

7 Cut the final thread ends to about 15cm (6in). (You may want to tie these thread ends together before cutting for extra security.) Take the ball thread end and slip it through the loop at the base of the ring. Take the shuttle thread end and slip it through the loop at the end of the chain [U].

U

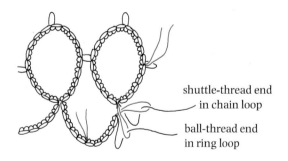

shuttle-thread end in chain loop

ball-thread end in ring loop

8 Pull the woven threads back through the stitches. This will automatically pull the final thread ends through the stitches as well [V].

V

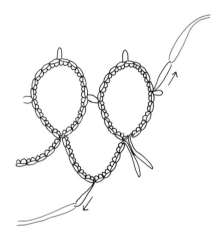

9 Make sure the final thread ends are completely pulled through the stitches. Now the thread ends are said to be woven into the work and are secure. Cut the ends close to the tatting for a neat finish [W].

W

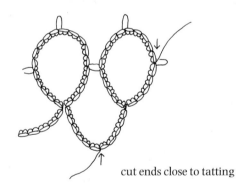

cut ends close to tatting

It is important to decide in advance whether or not to weave in the final ends, and if so, where. Some patterns, like the ring/chain pattern illustrated above, are fairly straightforward, but some are not so obvious.

If a pattern is a ring only pattern then there will be only one final end, but be careful about where this final end is woven.

Remember that this end is the anchor thread of the final ring just made, so if it is pulled back through the final stitches then the ring will unravel since the last stitches will no longer have an anchor thread! There are two solutions to this problem: either tie the thread end to the base of the ring before pulling it through the final stitches, or, better yet, avoid the final stitches altogether and weave the end into the *first* stitches of the final ring instead of the last [X].

Edging patterns, if put around a handkerchief or a doily, will end up back at their starting point. These patterns often *begin* with a ring and then end with a final chain joined to the base of the first ring. To finish off the ends, weave the shuttle thread into the last chain and the ball thread into either the first ring or the first chain. This takes a lot of forethought because one length of folded thread has to be woven into the first ring or first chain and left there till the work is completed. It's very frustrating to get all the way through and find you forgot to provide a place to weave in the final ends! If this does happen, however, both thread ends can be woven into the final chain, but sometimes this makes the final chain look noticeably thicker.

X

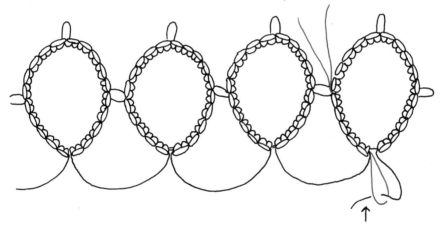

ring only pattern: thread end
woven into *first* stitches
of final ring

10

Half stitch techniques

Tatting does not have to be done with complete double stitches. If either half of the double stitch is repeated over and over a unique kind of tatting results. When repeating only one half of the double stitch the thread tends to become twisted more readily than if complete double stitches are repeated. Let the shuttle hang freely to allow the thread to untwist.

Josephine knots

Josephine knots are small rings made entirely of half stitches (either all first half or all second half stitches). These small rings are usually decorative, perhaps taking the place of decorative picots on a long chain.

1   Wind some thread onto a shuttle to practise making a josephine knot. Begin a ring with a first half stitch. Instead of completing the double stitch as usual, simply repeat the half stitch. Make 10 half stitches [A]. (Stitches in the diagram are shown very loose for clarity.)

2   Close the ring tightly. The completed ring is called a josephine knot. Normally, josephine knots do not have more than 10 or 12 half stitches, so they come out fairly small, with a very small centre hole.

3   Josephine knots can also be made using only second half stitches [B]. Once

A   josephine knot of first half stitches

before closing

after closing

completed it is very hard to tell which half of the double stitch was used to make a josephine knot.

4   Josephine knots are used mainly for decoration on chains, so patterns with josephine knots will nearly always require two shuttles. (It is basically a ring-on-a-chain pattern.) For practice, wind thread onto two shuttles. (Try using two different

B   josephine knot of second half stitches

before closing

after closing

Spiral tatting

As you have already seen, a half stitch repeated over and over in a ring results in a josephine knot. If the half stitches are made into a chain the result is called 'spiral tatting'.

1   Prepare shuttle and ball threads as you normally would for making a chain. Start with either a first or a second half stitch, then repeat the half stitch for a considerable length, say 30 times.

2   Push all the stitches together just as in a normal chain. Notice how the stitches will appear to spiral around the anchor thread [D].

D

colours to make things interesting.) Make a chain of three double stitches with shuttle one as anchor thread. Then, with shuttle two, make a josephine knot of 10 half stitches. Repeat the chain and josephine knot two more times, then end with three double stitches [C]. Notice how the josephine knots turn out to be the same colour as the chain because they are made with the working thread of the chain. The josephine knots should lie flat with no threads crossed.

C

Spiral chains have two important features. First, they are radially symmetric, meaning they look the same no matter how the chain is held. (Test this by holding a spiral chain at each end and rolling it. There is no obvious front and back as in a chain of normal double stitches.) The second important feature is that spiral chains do not curve like long chains of double stitches. Try making a chain of 15 double stitches, pushing the stitches close together, and compare it to your spiral chain of 30 half stitches. The spiral chain will be much more straight.

Sets of stitches

Another variation of half stitch tatting is 'sets of stitches', also known as 'node' or 'zigzag' stitching. Like spiral tatting, this technique is most commonly used to make long chains that do not curve.

1 Prepare shuttle and ball threads as you normally would for making a chain. Start the chain by making three first half stitches. Follow this with three second half stitches. All six half stitches counted together make one 'set' [E]. (Stitches in the diagram are shown very loose for clarity.)

E

set of stitches

one set   one set

2 Continue making sets of three first half/three second half stitches. Be sure to tighten the stitches so there are no gaps or picots. Notice how the chain does not automatically curve like a chain of double stitches would.

3 Look closely at the sets. Unlike spiral tatting, chains of sets look different depending on which side is viewed. Diagram F shows one side. The stitches appear to make a zigzag pattern, hence the name 'zigzag' stitching. Diagram G shows the reverse side of the chain. This view appears to be a smooth, straight thread with little

F

zigzag stitching

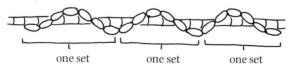

one set   one set   one set

nodes showing above and below it, hence the name 'node' stitching.

G   node stitching

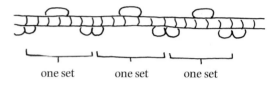

one set   one set   one set

4 Picots can be added to sets of stitches in the same way picots are added to normal chains. That is, a space left on the working thread between two half stitches will, when all the stitches are pushed together, result in a picot between those two half stitches. Be aware, however, that since the sets of stitches make a zigzag pattern the picots can be placed *either* at the top or the bottom of the chain. To illustrate, let's say you're making sets of three first half/three second half stitches. If you make a picot between *sets*, then all the picots will be on the same side of the chain, either at the top or bottom [H]. However, if you make a picot between

H

picots between sets

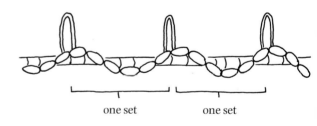

one set   one set

each *group* of three half stitches then the picots will be on both sides of the chain [I]. One case where picots would be wanted on one side only would be if a ring were being made of sets of stitches and picots were needed for joining. Picots on the inside of the

ring in this case would be of no use, so the
picots would only be put between sets [J].

I

J

picots between groups of half stitches

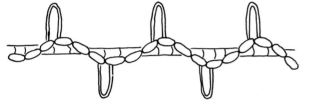

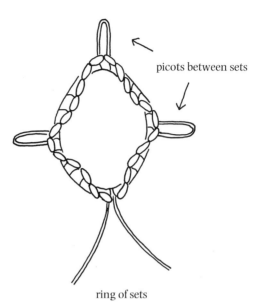

picots between sets

ring of sets

11

Decorative techniques

The techniques presented in this section do not require any new skills to be learned but they can add a lot of interest to otherwise standard patterns. All of these techniques are relatively rare, so there are no standard abbreviation or symbol instructions for them. When they are incorporated into a pattern the instructions will make it clear what is wanted.

Twisted picots

Most patterns have picots that are required for joining purposes. These picots are usually fairly small, just long enough to make the join and not be too conspicuous. However, picots used for joining can themselves be a feature of the tatting if the picot is made longer than normal and given a twist just before joining. To see the effect of twisted picots try making this very simple pattern:

1   Begin with a ring of [four double stitches, picot, (three double stitches, picot) 4 times, four double stitches, close]. Make all picots 6mm ($\frac{1}{4}$in) long. Remember that a 13mm ($\frac{1}{2}$in) space is required to make a 6mm ($\frac{1}{4}$in) picot. A piece of card 13mm ($\frac{1}{2}$in) wide can be used to measure the picots as they are made [A].

2   Once the ring is completed, reverse the work and make a chain of [(four double

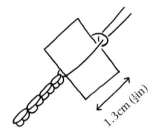

A

card held loosely in place
to measure a long picot

stitches, picot) three times, four double stitches]. The picots on the chain are decorative and can be any length.

3   Reverse the work and begin a second ring. Make five double stitches, then prepare to join the second ring to the 4th picot of Ring 1. Before making the join use a crochet hook to twist the picot [B].

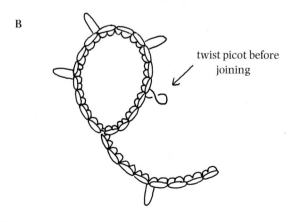

B

twist picot before
joining

4 After joining to the twisted picot, finish the second ring with five double stitches, close.

5 Repeat the chain and the second ring three more times, joining to the 3rd, 2nd, and then the 1st picot of Ring 1 respectively. Remember to twist each picot of Ring 1 just before joining each time. Join the final chain to the base of Ring 1 to complete the pattern [C]. (Very long picots can be twisted several times to give them a corded effect.)

C

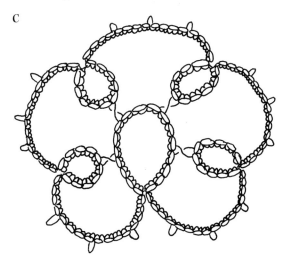

Half closed rings

This decorative technique is fairly self-explanatory. When a ring is completed it is only closed halfway, so that it makes a semi-circular shape [D]. Half closed rings are very useful because, unlike fully closed rings, they begin and end at different points. Fully closed rings made consecutively make a circular shape, like a clover motif, but half closed rings made consecutively make a linear shape, like an edging.

D

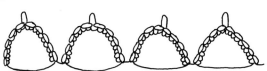

Netting

Netting is a ring only pattern that is so simple yet so interesting. Small rings alternate with long spaces in netting. Subsequent rows or rounds join the rings to the spaces [E]. In netting it is important to measure the spaces between the rings so that they are all made the correct length. Just as for twisted picots, a piece of card of the desired width can be used to measure the space. Usually the instructions will dictate the length that the spaces should be. Pay close attention because the spaces may get larger or smaller as the pattern progresses.

E

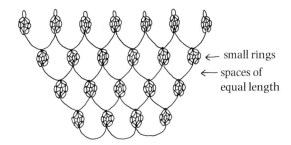

← small rings
← spaces of equal length

12

Reading patterns

Tatting has been around a long time, and the way tatting patterns are written has changed over the years. The main point is to study the pattern before taking even one stitch!

There are a few instructions in older patterns that may cause confusion. Look out for statements like the following:

Tie shuttle and ball threads together. This is not always necessary, as explained in the section on making chains. If you are working in one colour of thread then it is best to leave the shuttle thread attached to the ball at the beginning. This saves having ends to finish off later. If you are working in two colours (shuttle in one colour, ball in another), then obviously you cannot start with shuttle thread attached to the ball, but it is still not necessary to tie them together. Either weave in the ends as you start tatting or simply start tatting and finish off the ends later (see p. 50ff.).

Two shuttles required. Remember that two shuttles are needed only when both shuttle threads are going to be used as working threads (see p. 42).

All patterns specify size of thread to be used, but some will specify a certain manufacturer's thread. If the pattern is old the type of thread called for may not even be made anymore! Actually, only very rarely is

it necessary to use a specific make of thread, and even then, the reason should be given. For example, if metallic thread is being used then a certain brand name may be mentioned because there are so few metallic threads on the market suitable for tatting. Usually, however, if plain cotton thread is all that is required, then any make will do. Remember, however, that even amongst modern cotton threads different manufacturers make their sizes slightly different. So a size 20 in one make will be slightly thicker or thinner than a size 20 in another make. Therefore, even if you use the size thread called for in the pattern, the finished product may come out at slightly different dimensions than those quoted. This is also why it is not advisable to mix different makes of thread in one project.

Once you've sorted out the logistics of your chosen pattern (which thread to use, how many shuttles, etc.), then you have the task of actually following the stitch instructions. Unfortunately, instructions are not standardized so you have to learn several tatting 'languages'. Luckily, the languages are relatively similar. Also, at the beginning of every pattern, or book of patterns, there should be a glossary explaining terms, abbreviations, and symbols. *Read this section carefully* before beginning. The pattern section in this book starts with a typical list of abbreviations and symbols used in the patterns. For example 'ds' means double stitch, 'p' means picot, and 'cl' means close the ring. So a ring of [(4ds, p) 4 times, 4ds, cl] means make a ring of four double stitches, picot, four double stitches, picot, four double stitches, picot, four double stitches, picot, four double stitches, close. It's easy to see why abbreviations are much preferred over long hand!

More and more, modern tatters are choosing to *draw* the instructions for patterns rather than write out the instructions in abbreviations. Drawing has the advantage of the tatter being able to see the pattern instantly. Also, drawings can take up much less space and be clearer than a lengthy page of written instructions. On the other hand, instructions that are drawn do require that the tatter have a thorough understanding of tatting construction. For example, the tatter has to be able to tell just by looking at the picture that a reverse work

has been done between a ring and a chain, or that a josephine knot has been made as a ring-on-a-chain pattern and therefore requires two shuttles. These are the kinds of instructions that are spelled out in traditional written instructions, but are only implied in drawings.

To gain experience in reading drawings, as well as in tatting construction in general, it is advisable to start by drawing pictures of written instructions. That is, take any written pattern and, instead of tatting it, draw it first. This exercise will help you visualize the pattern more effectively than just reading through the written instructions. You'll see exactly how the pattern evolves, the order in which rings and chains are made and joined. Remember, the better you understand the construction of the pattern you're working on, the less likely you are to make mistakes in the actual tatting.

13

Patterns

Abbreviations and symbols

Ch = chain   p = picot
cl = close   prev. = previous
ds = double stitch R = ring
j = join   T = reverse work or turn
j.k. = josephine knot Sp = small picot
Lp = large picot

'Clover' is three rings made consecutively with no reverse work or chains in between. Usually the three rings are joined together.

'Measured picots' are picots of specified length which must be measured using a piece of card.

'Space' is a length of single thread left between two rings.

'Spacer' is a piece of card of specific width to 'measure' picots or spaces.

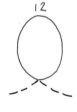

12 ds in a ring

space between two rings

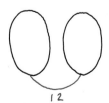

12 ds in a chain

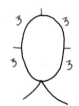

number of ds before and after picots in a ring

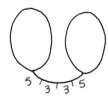

number of ds before and after picots in a chain

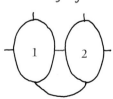

ring 2 is joined to ring 1 at 3rd picot (of ring 1)

Edgings

Ring only edging (1)

Techniques: rings, large and small picots, joins

Materials: 1 shuttle, size 10 thread

Measurements: 2cm (¾in) wide

R1 (large ring): 5ds, Lp, 3ds, p, 3ds, Lp, 5ds, cl.

* R2: 6ds, Sp, 3ds, p, 3ds, cl. Leave a space of thread *behind* R2, then join to Sp of R2.

R3: 5ds, j to last p of prev. large ring, 3ds, p, 3ds, Lp, 5ds, cl.

Repeat from * to length desired.

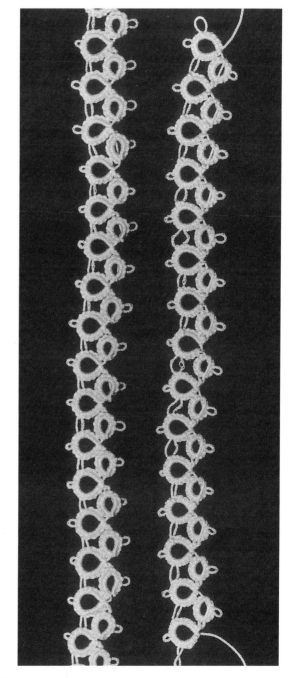

2   Ring only edging (1) – front view (*left*) and back view (*right*)

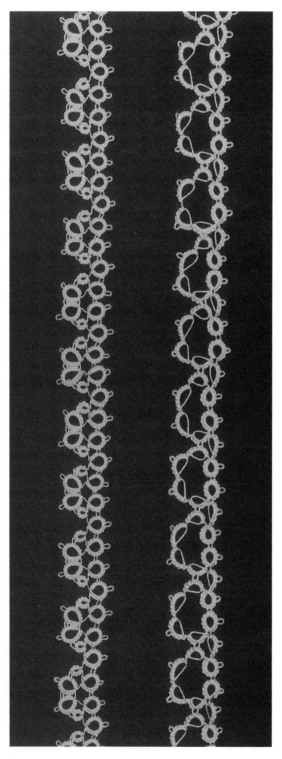

Ring only edging (2)

Techniques: rings, joins, reverse work (turn)
Materials: 1 shuttle, size 40 thread
Measurement: 1.5cm ($\frac{5}{8}$in) wide

Note: 'small space' is a length of thread 3mm ($\frac{1}{8}$in) long

R1 (med. ring): 4ds, p, 4ds, p, 4ds, p, 4ds, cl, T, small space.

* R2 (small ring): 4ds, p, 4ds, cl, T, small space.

R3 (med. ring): 4ds, j to 3rd p of prev. med. ring, 4ds, p, 4ds, p, 4ds, cl, T, small space.

R4 (large ring): 5ds, j to p of prev. small ring, 4ds, p, 4ds, p, 5ds, cl.

R5 (large ring): 5ds, j to last p of prev. ring, 4ds, p, 4ds, p, 5ds, cl, T, small space.

R6 (med. ring): 4ds, j to 3rd p of prev. med. ring, 4ds, p, 4ds, p, 4ds, cl, T, small space.

R7 (small ring): 4ds, j to last p of R5, 4ds, cl, T, small space.

R8 (med. ring): 4ds, j to 3rd p of prev. med. ring, 4ds, p, 4ds, p, 4ds, cl, T, small space.

Repeat from * to length desired.

3a   Ring only edging (2) (*left*)

3b   Ring only edging with half-closed rings (*right*)

Ring only edging with half-closed rings

Techniques: rings, half-closed rings, reverse
  work (turn)
Materials: 1 shuttle, size 40 thread
Measurements: 2cm (¾in) wide

R1: 3ds, p, 3ds, p, 6ds, cl, T.
R2: 3ds, p, 3ds, half-close.
* R3: 4ds, p, 4ds, half-close.
R4: 4ds, p, 4ds, half-close.
R5: 3ds, p, 3ds, half-close, T.
R6: 6ds, j to 2nd p of R1, 3ds, p, 3ds, cl.
R7: 3ds, p, 3ds, half-close.
R8 (same as R1): 3ds, p, 3ds, p, 6ds, cl, T.
R9: 3ds, j to p of prev. R5, 3ds, half-close.

Repeat from * to length desired.

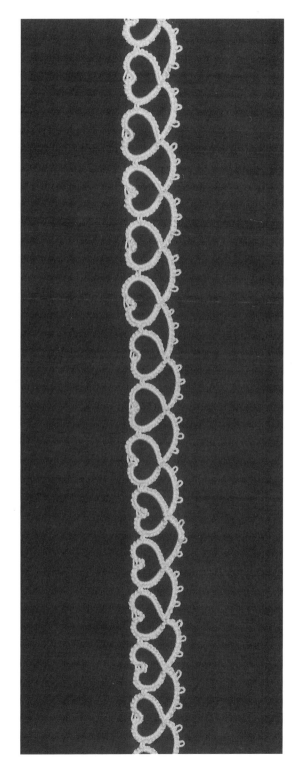

Heart edging

Techniques: rings, chains, joins, reverse
  work (turn)
Materials: 1 shuttle, 1 ball, size 10 thread
Measurements: 2cm (¾in) wide

R1: 9ds, p, 6ds, p, 5ds, j to last p, 6ds, p, 9ds,
  cl, T.
* Ch1: 3ds, p, 3ds, p, 3ds, p, 3ds, T.
R2: 9ds, j to last p of prev. R, 6ds, p, 5ds, j to
  prev. p, 6ds, p, 9ds, cl, T.

Repeat from * to length desired.

4   Heart edging

Two shuttle edging with corner

Techniques: rings, chains, joins, reverse
    work (turn), two shuttle tatting
Materials: 2 shuttles, size 20 thread
Measurements: 3cm ($1\frac{1}{8}$in) wide

Note: Shuttles designated hold the *working
thread* for that ring or chain

Straight edging
(Shuttle 1)   R1: 5ds, p, 5ds, p, 5ds, p, 5ds, cl.

5a   Two shuttle edging with corner (*left*)

5b   Two shuttle edging with josephine knots
(*right*)

R2: 5ds, p, 5ds, p, 5ds, p, 5ds,
    cl, T.
(Shuttle 2)   Ch1: 9ds, p, 3ds.
(Shuttle 2) * R3: 5ds, p, 5ds, p, 5ds, cl, T.
(Shuttle 1)   Ch2: 6ds, j to 2nd p of R2, 3ds.
(Shuttle 1)   R4: 5ds, j to 1st p of R2, 5ds, p,
    5ds, p, 5ds, cl.
R5: Repeat R2.
(Shuttle 2)   Ch3: 9ds, j to 2nd p of R3, 3ds.

Repeat from * to length desired.

Corner
Make straight edging up to Ch3, then:
(Shuttle 2) Ch3: 9ds, j to 2nd p of R3, 3ds, p,
    1ds, T.

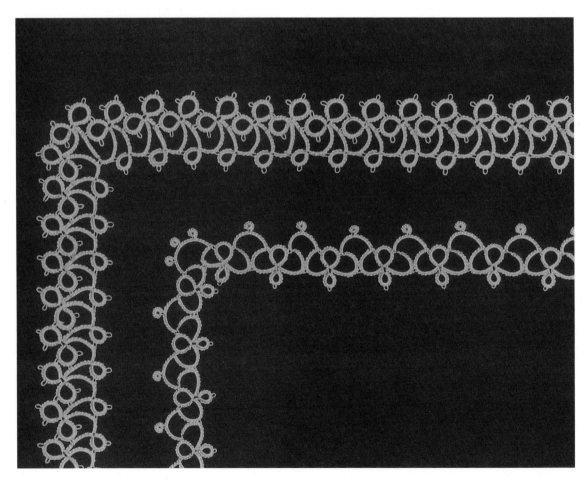

(Shuttle 1) Ch4: 6ds, j to 2nd p of R2, 3ds.
(Shuttle 1) R5: 5ds, j to 1st p of R2, 5ds, p,
     5ds, p, 5ds, cl.
     R6: 5ds, p, 5ds, p, 5ds, p, 5ds, cl, T.
(Shuttle 2) Ch5: 10ds, T.
(Shuttle 1) R7: 5ds, j to 2nd p of R6, 5ds, p,
     5ds, p, 5ds, cl.
     R8 (same as R2 of straight
     portion): 5ds, p, 5ds, p, 5ds,
     p, 5ds, cl, T.
(Shuttle 2) Ch6: 9ds, j to p of Ch3, 3ds.

Continue with straight edging from *.

Two shuttle edging with josephine knots

Techniques: rings, chains, joins, reverse
    work (turn), two shuttle tatting,
    josephine knots
Materials: 2 shuttles, size 20 thread
Measurements: 2.5cm (1in) wide

Note: Shuttle designated holds the *working
thread* for that ring or chain.

Straight edging
(Shuttle 1)   R1: 6ds, p, 8ds, p, 6ds, cl, T.
(Shuttle 2)   R2: 6ds, p, 6ds, cl.
(Shuttle 2)   Ch1: 8ds, p, 8ds, j using
    anchor thread to 2nd p of
    R1, T.

(Shuttle 1)   Ch2 with j.k.: 7ds, j.k. of 10
    half stitches using shuttle
    1, 7ds, p, 1ds, T.
(Shuttle 2)   Ch3: 7ds, j to p of Ch1, 8ds, T.
(Shuttle 1)   R3: 6ds, j to p of Ch2, 8ds, p,
    6ds, cl, T.
(Shuttle 2)   * R4: 6ds, p, 6ds, cl.
(Shuttle 2)   Ch4: 8ds, p, 8ds, j using anchor
    thread to p of prev. R3, T.
(Shuttle 1)   Ch5 with j.k.: 7ds, j.k. of 10
    half stitches using shuttle
    1, 7ds, p, 1ds, T.
(Shuttle 2)   Ch6: 7ds, j to p of Ch4, 8ds, T.
(Shuttle 1)   R5: 6ds, j to p of Ch5, 8ds, p,
    6ds, cl, T.

Repeat from * to length desired.

Corner
Make straight edging up to Ch4, then:
(Shuttle 2) Ch4: 6ds, p, 6ds, j using anchor
    thread to p of prev. R3, T.
(Shuttle 1) Ch5 with j.k.s: 5ds, j.k. of 10 half
    stitches using shuttle 1, 5ds,
    j.k. of 10 half stitches using
    shuttle 1, 5ds, j.k. of 10 half
    stitches using shuttle 1, 5ds,
    p, 1ds, T.
(Shuttle 2) Ch6: 5ds, j to p of Ch4 of corner,
    6ds, T.
(Shuttle 1) R: 6ds, j to p of Ch6 of corner,
    8ds, p, 6ds, cl, T.

Continue with straight edging from *.

Inserts

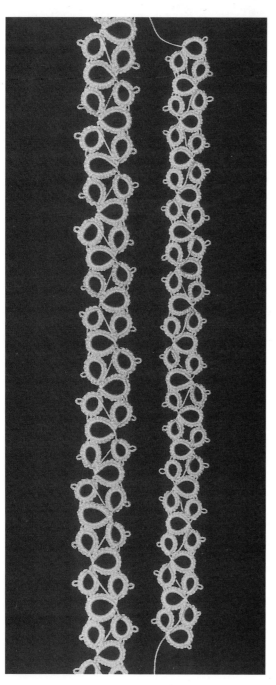

Ring only insert

Techniques: rings, joins, reverse work (turn)
Materials: 1 shuttle, either size 10 or size 20 thread
Measurements: size 10 thread: 2.2cm ($\frac{7}{8}$in) wide; size 20 thread: 2cm ($\frac{3}{4}$in) wide

R1: 8ds, p, 5ds, p, 8ds, cl, T.
* R2: 4ds, p, 4ds, p, 8ds, cl, T, space of approx. 13mm ($\frac{1}{2}$in).
R3: 8ds, j to 2nd p of R1, 4ds, p, 4ds, cl, T.
R4: 8ds, j to 2nd p of R2, 5ds, p, 8ds, cl, T.

Repeat from * to length desired.

6   Ring only insert: size 10 thread (*left*) and size 20 thread (*right*)

Two row insert (1)

Techniques: rings, chains, joins, reverse
    work (turn)
Materials: 1 shuttle, 1 ball, size 40 thread
Measurements: 3.5cm (1⅜in) wide

1st row

Clover: R1: 4ds, p, 4ds, p, 4ds, p, 4ds, cl.
       R2: 4ds, j to last p of prev. R, 6ds, p,
           6ds, p, 4ds, cl.
       R3: 4ds, j to last p of prev. R, 4ds, p,
           4ds, p, 4ds, cl, T.

*Ch1: 4ds, p, 4ds, p, 4ds, p, 4ds, p, 4ds, T.

Clover: R1: 4ds, p, 4ds, j to 2nd p of last ring
          of prev. clover, 4ds, p, 4ds, cl.
       R2: 4ds, j to last p of prev. R, 6ds, p,
           6ds, p, 4ds, cl.
       R3: 4ds, j to last p of prev. R, 4ds, p,
           4ds, p, 4ds, cl, T.

Repeat from * to length desired.

2nd row

2nd row is made exactly as 1st row, with
the centre R of each clover joined to a 1st
row clover as shown in diagram A.

A

2nd row

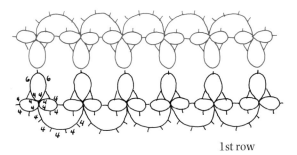

1st row

Two row insert (2)

Techniques: rings, chains, joins, reverse
     work (turn)
Materials: 1 shuttle, 1 ball, size 40 thread
Measurements: 3.5cm (1$\frac{3}{8}$in) wide

Follow the diagram for 1st row:

B

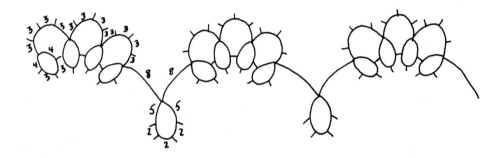

Follow the diagram for 2nd row, joining to
1st row as shown:

C

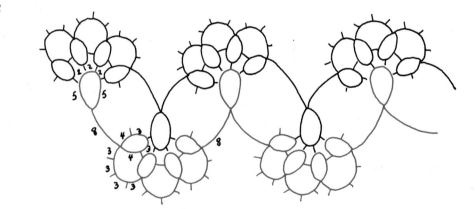

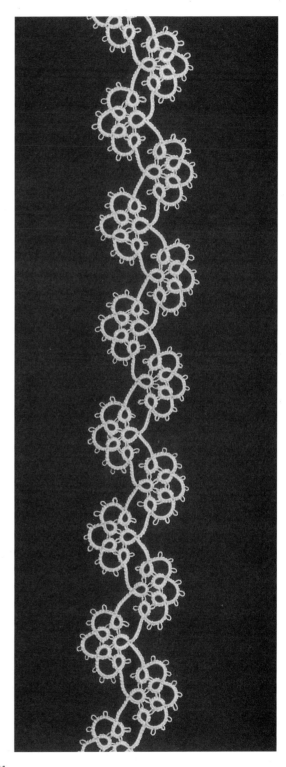

8   Two row insert (2)

Flower insert

Techniques: rings. chains, joins, reverse
   work (turn), two shuttle tatting
Materials: 2 shuttles, size 40 thread
Measurements: 4cm (1⅝in) wide

1st 'flower'

All rings made with shuttle 1 and all chains
made with shuttle 2 as working thread.
R1: 8ds, p, 3ds, p, 8ds, cl, T.
Ch1: 3ds, p, 3ds, p, 3ds, p, 3ds, T.
* R2: 8ds, j to last p of prev. R, 3ds, p, 8ds, cl,
   T.
Ch2: 3ds, p, 3ds, p, 3ds, p, 3ds, T.

Repeat from * 3 times, ending with Ch5.

R6: 8ds, j to last p of prev. R, 3ds, j to first p
   of R1, cl, T.

2nd 'flower'

This is made exactly as the first flower,
except all rings are made with shuttle 2 and
all chains are made with shuttle 1 as
working thread.

3rd 'flower'

All rings made with shuttle 1 and all chains
made with shuttle 2 as working thread.
R1: 8ds, p, 3ds, p, 8ds, cl, T.
Ch1: 3ds, p, 3ds, j to center p of Ch5 of 1st
   flower, 3ds, p, 3ds, T.
* R2: 8ds, j to last p of prev. R, 3ds, p, 8ds, cl,
   T.
Ch2: 3ds, p, 3ds, p, 3ds, p, 3ds, T.

Repeat from * 3 times, ending with Ch5.

R6: 8ds, j to last p of prev. R, 3ds, j to first p
   of R1, cl, T.

4th 'Flower'

This is made exactly as the 3rd flower,
except all rings are made with shuttle 2 and
all chains are made with shuttle 1 as
working thread, and Ch1 is joined to Ch5 of
the 2nd flower.

See diagram D for order in which flowers are
made and joined. Also note that shuttle 1
thread is a different colour from shuttle 2
thread.

D

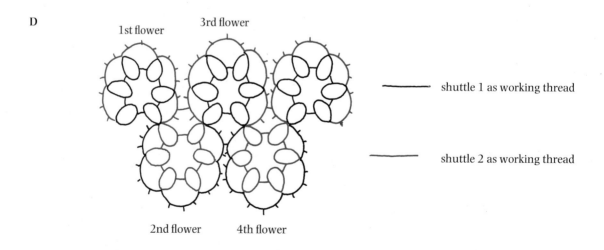

1st flower   3rd flower

——————   shuttle 1 as working thread

——————   shuttle 2 as working thread

2nd flower   4th flower

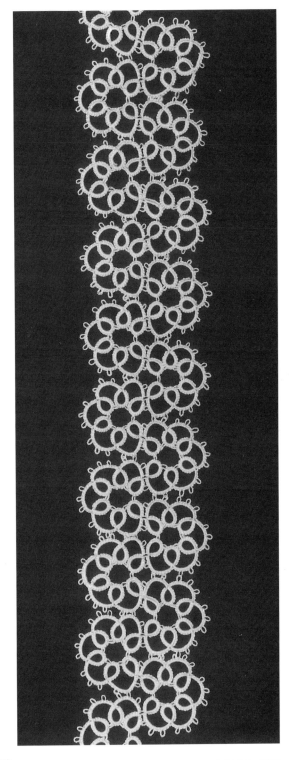

9   Flower insert

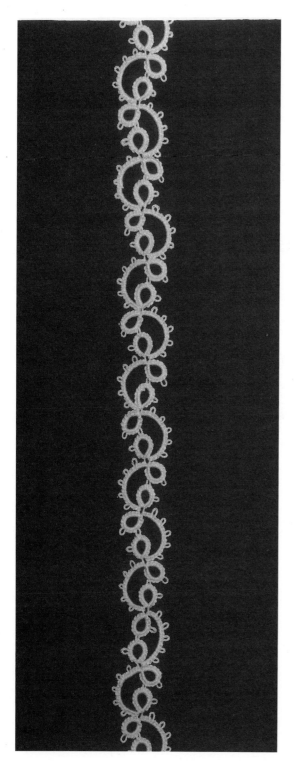

Two shuttle insert

Techniques: rings, chains, joins, reverse
      work (turn), two shuttle tatting
Materials: 2 shuttles, size 20 thread
Measurements: 2cm ($\frac{3}{4}$in) wide

Note: Shuttle designated holds the *working
thread* for that ring or chain.

(Shuttle 1)   R1: 4ds, p, 4ds, p, 8ds, cl, T.
(Shuttle 2)   Ch1: (3ds, p) 5 times, 3ds, T.
(Shuttle 1) * R2: 4ds, j to 2nd p of prev. R,
                  4ds, p, 8ds, cl. T.
(Shuttle 2)   R3: 4ds, p, 4ds, p, 8ds, cl, T.
(Shuttle 1)   Ch2: (3ds, p) 5 times, 3ds, T.
(Shuttle 2)   R4: 4ds, j to 2nd p of prev. R,
                  4ds, p, 8ds, cl, T.
(Shuttle 1)   R5: 4ds, p, 4ds, p, 8ds, cl, T.
(Shuttle 2)   Ch4: (3ds, p) 5 times, 3ds, T.

Repeat from * to length desired.

10   Two shuttle insert

Motifs

Cross

Techniques: rings, chains, joins, large picot,
reverse work (turn)
Materials: 1 shuttle, 1 ball, size 20 thread
Measurements: 10.5cm (4¼in) high; 7.5cm
(3in) wide

Note: 'CM' means 'Centre motif'.

Centre motif

R1: 2ds, p, 5ds, p, 4ds, p, 5ds, p, 2ds, cl.
R2: 2ds, j to last p of prev. R, 5ds, p, 4ds, p,
5ds, p, 2ds, cl.
R3: same as R2.
R4: 2ds, j to last p of prev. R, 5ds, p, 4ds, p,
5ds, j to 1st p of R1, 2ds, cl. Cut and
finish ends.

Round

R1: 5ds, j to 3rd p of any R of CM, 4ds, p,
5ds, cl, T.
* Ch1: 12ds, T.
R2: 8ds, j to free p of prev. R, 8ds, cl.
R3: 8ds, Lp, 8ds, cl, T.
Ch2: 15ds, T.
R4: 6ds, j to Lp of R3, 6ds, cl, T.
Ch3: 12ds, T.
R5: 6ds, j to Lp of R3, 6ds, cl, T.
Ch4: 15ds, T.
R6: 8ds, j to Lp of R3, 8ds, cl.
R7: 8ds, p, 8ds, cl, T.
Ch5: 12ds, T.
R8: 5ds, j to p of prev. R, 4ds, j to free p of
same R of CM as R1, 5ds, cl, T.
Ch6: 2ds, T.
R9: 5ds, j to next free p of CM, 4ds, p, 5ds, cl,
T.

Repeat from * *twice.*

11   Cross

Ch7: 12ds, T.
R10: 8ds, j to free p of prev. R, 8ds, cl.
R11: 8ds, p, 8ds, cl, T.
Ch8: 15ds, T.
R12 (ring a of clover): 6ds, j to p of prev. R,
6ds, cl.
R13 (ring b of clover): 6ds, p, 6ds, cl.
R14 (ring c of clover): 6ds, p, 6ds, cl, T.
Ch9: 15ds, T.
R15: 8ds, j to p of prev. R, 8ds, cl.
R16: 8ds, Lp, 8ds, cl, T.
Ch10: 12ds, T.

R17: 6ds, j to Lp of R16, 6ds, cl, T.
Ch11: 12ds, T.
R18: 6ds, j to Lp of R16, 6ds, cl, T.
Ch12: 12ds, T.
R19: 8ds, j to Lp of R16, 8ds, cl.
R20: 8ds, p, 8ds, cl, T.
Ch13: 15ds, T.
R21: 6ds, j to p of prev. R, 6ds, cl, j to p of
    R13 (ring b of clover).
R22: 6ds, p, 6ds, cl, T.
Ch14: 15ds, T.
R23: 8ds, j to p of prev. R, 8ds, cl.
R24: 8ds, p, 8ds, cl, T.
Ch15: 12ds, T.
R25: 5ds, j to p of prev. R, 4ds, j to last free p
    of CM, 5ds, cl, T.
Ch16: 2ds, j to base of R1. Cut and finish
    ends.

Heart

Techniques: rings, chains, joins, reverse
  work (turn)
Materials: 1 shuttle, 1 ball, size 20 thread
Measurements: approx. 5cm (2in)

1st round

Clover 1 R1: (2ds, p) 8 times, 2ds, cl.
  R2: 2ds, j to last p of R1, (2ds, p) 10
    times, 2ds, cl.
  R3: 2ds, j to last p of R2, (2ds, p) 7
    times, 2ds, cl, T.

Ch1: 10ds, T.

Clover 2 R4: (2ds, p) 3 times, 2ds, j to 5th p
    of R3, (2ds, p) 4 times, 2ds, cl.
  R5: 2ds, j to last p of R4, (2ds, p) 10
    times, 2ds, cl.

R6: 2ds, j to last p of R5, (2ds, p) 7
    times, 2ds, cl, T.

Ch2: 10ds, T.

Clover 3 R7: (2ds, p) 5 times, 2ds, cl.
  R8: (2ds, p) 9 times, 2ds, cl.
  R9: (2ds, p) 5 times, 2ds, cl, T.

Ch3: 10ds, j to base of clover 1.
Cut and finish ends.

2nd round

R1: 5ds, j to 3rd p of R3, 3ds, j to 9th p of
  R2, 5ds, cl, T.
Ch1: (2ds, p) 4 times, 2ds, T.
R2: 5ds, j to 7th p of R2, 5ds, cl, T.
Ch2: (2ds, p) 4 times, 2ds, T.
R3: 5ds, j to 5th p of R2, 5ds, cl, T.

12   Heart

Ch3: (2ds, p) 4 times, 2ds, T.
R4: 5ds, j to 6th p of R1, 5ds, cl, T.
Ch4: (2ds, p) 4 times, 2ds, T.
R5: 5ds, j to 4th p of R1, 2ds, j to 3rd p of
    R9, 5ds, cl, T.
Ch5: (2ds, p) 3 times, 2ds, T.
R6: 3ds, j to 7th p of R8, 3ds, cl, T.
Ch6: (2ds, p) 3 times, 2ds, T.
R7: 3ds, j to 5th p of R8, 3ds, cl, T.
Ch7: (2ds, p) 3 times, 2ds, T.
R8: 3ds, j to 3rd p of R8, 3ds, cl, T.
Ch8: (2ds, p) 3 times, 2ds, T.

R9: 5ds, j to 3rd p of R7, 2ds, j to 5th p of
    R6, 5ds, cl, T.
Ch9: (2ds, p) 4 times, 2ds, T.
R10: 5ds, j to 3rd p of R6, 5ds, cl, T.
Ch10: (2ds, p) 4 times, 2ds, T.
R11: 5ds, j to 7th p of R5, 5ds, cl, T.
Ch11: (2ds, p) 4 times, 2ds, T.
R12: 5ds, j to 5th p of R5, 5ds, cl, T.
Ch12: (2ds, p) 4 times, 2ds, T.
R13: 5ds, j to 3rd p of R5, 3ds, j to 6th p of
    R4, 5ds, cl.
Cut and finish ends.

Star

Techniques: rings, chains, large and small picots, reverse work (turn), two shuttle tatting

Materials: 2 shuttles, size 20 thread

Measurements: 6.5cm (2½in)

Note: Shuttle designated holds *working thread* for that ring or chain.

Centre motif using two shuttles

(Shuttle 1)   R1: 8ds, Lp, 8ds, cl, T.
(Shuttle 2)   Ch1: 5ds.
(Shuttle 2)   R2 (Ring-on-chain): 6ds, p, 6ds, cl.
(Shuttle 2)   Ch2: 4ds.
(Shuttle 2)   R3 (Ring-on-chain): 6ds, p, 6ds, cl.
(Shuttle 2)   Ch3: 5ds, T.
(Shuttle 1) * R4: 8ds, j to Lp of R1, 8ds, cl, T.
(Shuttle 2)   Repeat Ch1, R2, Ch2, R3, Ch3.

Repeat from * 3 times, joining last chain to base of first ring. Cut and finish ends.

Clover motifs using one shuttle

R1: 6ds, j to R2 of centre motif, 5ds, Sp, 1ds, cl.
R2: 1ds, j to Sp of R1, 7ds, p, 7ds, Sp, cl.
R3: 1ds, j to Sp of R2, 5ds, j to next ring-on-chain of centre motif, 6ds, cl. Cut and finish ends.

Repeat clover motif *four* times.

13   Star

Snowflake

Techniques: rings, chains, joins, reverse
    work (turn), two shuttle tatting
Materials: 2 shuttles, size 40 thread
Measurements: 7.5cm (3in)

Note: Shuttle designated holds *working
thread* for that ring or chain.

14   Snowflake

Centre ring
(3ds, p) 11 times, 3ds, cl, T.

First 'arm' of snowflake
(See diagram E for order of rings)
        Ch1: 5ds, p, 5ds, T.
(Shuttle 1) * R1: 3ds, p, 3ds, cl, T.
(Shuttle 2)   Ch2: 4ds.
(Shuttle 2)   R2 (ring-on-chain): (1ds, p) 5
        times, 1ds, cl.
(Shuttle 2)   Ch3: 4ds, T.

(Shuttle 1) R3: (1ds, p) 7 times, 1ds, cl, T.
(Shuttle 2) Ch4: 7ds.
(Shuttle 2) R4 (ring-on-chain): (1ds, p) 5
      times, 1ds, cl.
(Shuttle 2) Ch5: 7ds, j to 4th p of R3 using
      anchor thread, 4ds.
(Shuttle 2) R5 (ring-on-chain): (1ds, p) 5
      times, 1ds, cl.
(Shuttle 2) Ch6: 4ds, T.
(Shuttle 1) R6: 3ds, j to p of R1, 3ds, cl, T.
(Shuttle 2) Ch7: 5ds, p, 5ds, j to next p of
      centre ring using anchor
      thread, 2ds, j to next p of
      centre ring using anchor
      thread, 5ds, j to free p of
      Ch7, 5ds, T.

Repeat from * 5 times with final chain as
follows:

Final chain: 5ds, j to p of Ch1, 5ds, j to next
   p of centre ring, 2ds, j to base of centre
   ring. Cut and finish ends.

E

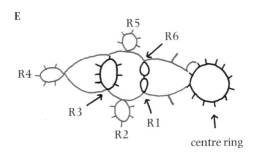

    —————— shuttle 1 as working thread

    —————— shuttle 2 as working thread

Butterfly

Techniques: rings, chains, joins (including joining into a previously made join), reverse work (turn), two shuttle tatting
Materials: 2 shuttles, size 40 thread
Measurements: 6.5cm (2½in) wide; 5cm (2in) high

Note: All rings are made with shuttle 1 as working thread and all chains are made with shuttle 2 as working thread unless otherwise stated.

Centre ring or 'body'

3ds, p, 3ds, p, (4ds, p) 6 times, 3ds, p, 3ds, cl, T.

Ch1: 10ds, T.
R1: 5ds, p, 5ds, cl, T.
Ch2: (2ds, p) 5 times, 2ds, j to p of R1 using anchor thread, 10ds, j to next p of centre ring using anchor thread, 10ds, j into prev. j to R1 using working thread, T.
R2: 5ds, p, 5ds, cl, T.
Ch3: (2ds, p) 5 times, 2ds, j to p of R2 using anchor thread, 6ds, p, 4ds, j to next p of centre ring using anchor thread, 4ds, j to prev. p, 6ds, T.
R3: 5ds, p, 5ds, cl, T.
Ch4: 6ds, T.
R4: 8ds, p, 8ds, cl, T.
Ch5: (2ds, p) 8 times, 2ds, j to p of R4 using anchor thread, 6ds, j to p of R3 using anchor thread, 10ds, j to next p of centre ring using anchor thread, 10ds, j into prev. j to R3 using working thread, T.
R5: 5ds, p, 5ds, cl, T.
Ch6: 6ds, j to prev. j to R4 using working thread, T.
R6: 8ds, p, 8ds, cl, T.
Ch7: (2ds, p) 8 times, 2ds, j to p of R6 using anchor thread, 6ds, j to p of R5 using anchor thread, 10ds, j to next p of centre

ring using anchor thread, 10ds, j into prev. j to R5 using working thread, T.
R7: 5ds, p, 5ds, cl, T.
Ch8: 6ds, j into prev. j to R6 using working thread, T.
R8: 8ds, p, 8ds, cl, T.
Ch9: (2ds, p) 8 times, 2ds, j to p of R8 using anchor thread, 6ds, j to p of R7 using anchor thread, 10ds, j to next p of centre ring using anchor thread.

Ring 9 or 'head'

(Shuttle 2) 7ds, 3.2cm (1¼in) picot, 7ds, cl.

Ch10: 10ds, T.
R10: 5ds, p, 5ds, cl, T.
Ch11: 6ds, T.
R11: 8ds, p, 8ds, cl, T.
Ch12: (2ds, p) 8 times, 2ds, j to p of R11 using anchor thread, 6ds, j to p of R10 using anchor thread, 10ds, j to next p of centre ring using anchor thread, 10ds, j into prev. j to R10 using working thread, T.
R12: 5ds, p, 5ds, cl, T.
Ch13: 6ds, j into prev. j to R11 using working thread, T.
R13: 8ds, p, 8ds, cl, T.
Ch14: (2ds, p) 8 times, 2ds, j to p of R13 using anchor thread, 6ds, j to p of R12 using anchor thread, 10ds, j to next p of centre ring using anchor thread, 10ds, j into prev. j to R12 using working thread, T.
R14: 5ds, p, 5ds, cl, T.
Ch15: 6ds, j into prev. j to R13 using working thread, T.
R15: 8ds, p, 8ds, cl, T.
Ch16: (2ds, p) 8 times, j to p of R15 using anchor thread, 6ds, j to p of R14 using anchor thread, 6ds, p, 4ds, j to next p of centre ring using anchor thread, 4ds, j to prev. p, 6ds, T.

R16: 5ds, p, 5ds, cl, T.

Ch17: (2ds, p) 5 times, 2ds, j to p of R16
using anchor thread, 10ds, j to next p of
centre ring using anchor thread, 10ds, j
into prev. j to R16 using working
thread, T.

R17: 5ds, p, 5ds, cl, T.

Ch18: (2ds, p) 5 times, 2ds, j to p of R17
using anchor thread, 10ds, j to base of
centre ring.

Cut and finish ends.

Cut long picot on head to make antennae.   15   Butterfly

Mats

Small mat

Techniques: rings, chains, joins (including joining into a previously made join), reverse work (turn)
Materials: 1 shuttle, 1 ball, size 20 thread
Measurements: 10cm (4in) diameter

Centre motif

R1: 7ds, p, 3ds, p, 6ds, p, 3ds, p, 7ds, cl.
R2: 7ds, j to last p of prev. R, 3ds, p, 6ds, p, 3ds, p, 7ds, cl.
Repeat R2 *three* times to make R3, R4, and R5.
R6: 7ds, j to last p of prev. R, 3ds, p, 6ds, p, 3ds, j to first p of R1, 7ds, cl, j to base of R1. Cut and finish ends.

Rounds of chains

1st round: j to any p of centre motif, * 5ds, j to next p of centre motif using anchor thread, repeat from * to finish round. DO NOT BREAK THREAD.
2nd round: * 7ds, j into next previously made join using anchor thread, repeat from * to finish round. DO NOT BREAK THREAD.
3rd round: * 9ds, j into next previously made join using anchor thread, repeat from * to finish round. DO NOT BREAK THREAD.
4th round: * (3ds, p) 3 times, 3ds, j into next previously made join using anchor thread, repeat from * to finish round. Cut and finish ends.
5th round: R1: 5ds, p, 5ds, p, 3ds, j to middle p of any chain in 4th round, 3ds, p, 5ds, p, 5ds, cl, T. * Ch1: 5ds, p, 7ds, p, 5ds, T.

16   Small mat

R2: 5ds, p, 5ds, p, 3ds, j to middle p of next chain in 4th round, 3ds, p, 5ds, p, 5ds, cl, T.

Repeat from * to finish round. Cut and finish ends.

Rounds of chains

6th round: j to any p of 5th round, * 9ds, j to next p of 5th round using anchor thread, repeat from * to finish round. DO NOT BREAK THREAD.
7th round: * 11ds, j into next previously made join using anchor thread, repeat from * to finish round. DO NOT BREAK THREAD.
8th round: * 4ds, p, 5ds, p, 4ds, j into next previously made join using anchor thread, repeat from * to finish round. Cut and finish ends.

Ring only mat

Techniques: rings, joins, large picot, reverse work (turn), measured spaces
Materials: 1 shuttle, 6mm ($\frac{1}{4}$in) spacer, size 40 thread
Measurements: 18.5cm ($7\frac{1}{2}$in) diameter

Note: All spaces are 6mm ($\frac{1}{4}$in).

Centre ring
2ds, p, (3ds, p) 11 times, 1ds, cl. Cut and finish ends.

1st round
R1: 5ds, j to any p of centre ring, 5ds, cl, T, space.
R2: (large ring): 5ds, p, (3ds, p) 8 times, 5ds, cl, T, space.

17   Ring only mat

R3: 5ds, j to next p of centre ring, 5ds, cl, T, space.
* R4 (large ring): 5ds, j to last p of prev. large ring, (3ds, p) 8 times, 5ds, cl, T, space.
R5: 5ds, j to next p of centre ring, 5ds, cl, T, space.

Repeat from * 9 times.

Final large ring
5ds, j to last p of prev. large ring, (3ds, p) 7 times, 3ds, j to 1st p of first large ring (R2), 5ds, cl, T, space, join to base of R1. Cut and finish ends.

2nd round
R1: 5ds, j to 4th p of any 1st round large ring, 5ds, cl, T, space.
R2 (large ring): 5ds, p, (3ds, p) 8 times, 5ds, cl, T, space.

R3: 5ds, j to 6th p of same 1st round large ring, 5ds, cl, T, space.

* R4 (large ring): 5ds, j to last p of prev. large ring, (3ds, p) 8 times, 5ds, cl, T, space.

R5: 5ds, j to 4th p of next 1st round large ring, 5ds, cl, T, space.

R6 (large ring): 5ds, j to last p of prev. large ring, (3ds, p) 8 times, 5ds, cl, T, space.

R7: 5ds, j to 6th p of same 1st round large ring, 5ds, cl, T, space.

Repeat from * 10 times.

Final large ring

5ds, j to last p of prev. large ring, (3ds, p) 7 times, 3ds, j to 1st p of first large ring (R2), 5ds, cl, T, space, j to base of R1. Cut and finish ends.

3rd round

R1: 5ds, j to 6th p of any 2nd round large ring, 5ds, cl, T, space.

R2: 5ds, Lp, 5ds, cl, T, space.

R3: 5ds, j to 4th p of next 2nd round large ring, 5ds, cl, T, space.

R4: 5ds, j to prev. Lp, 5ds, cl, T, space.

* R5: 5ds, j to 6th p of same 2nd round large ring, 5ds, cl, T, space.

R6: 5ds, Lp, 5ds, cl, T, space.

R7: 5ds, j to 4th p of next 2nd round large ring, 5ds, cl, T, space.

R8: 5ds, j to prev. Lp, 5ds, cl, T, space.

Repeat from * 22 times, ending by joining to the base of R1. Cut and finish ends.

4th round

R1: 5ds, j to any Lp of 3rd round, 5ds, cl, T, space.

R2 (medium ring): (3ds, p) 7 times, 3ds, cl, T, space.

R3: 5ds, j to same Lp of 3rd round, 5ds, cl, T, space.

* R4 (large ring): 5ds, p, 3ds, j to 6th p of prev.

medium ring, (3ds, p) 7 times, 5ds, cl, T, space

R5: 5ds, j to next Lp of 3rd round, 5ds, cl, T, space.

R6 (medium ring): 3ds, p, 3ds, j to 8th p of prev. large ring, (3ds, p) 5 times, 3ds, cl, T, space.

R7: 5ds, j to same Lp of 3rd round, 5ds, cl, T, space.

Repeat from * 22 times.

Final large ring

5ds, p, 3ds, j to 6th p of prev. medium ring, (3ds, p) 5 times, 3ds, j to 2nd p of 1st medium ring (R2), 3ds, p, 5ds, cl, T, space, j to base of R1. Cut and finish ends.

5th round

R1: 5ds, j to 4th p of any 4th round large ring, 5ds, cl, T, space.

R2 (small ring): 3ds, p, 3ds, cl, T, space.

R3: 5ds, j to 6th p of same 4th round large ring, 5ds, cl, T, space.

R4 (large ring): 3ds, j to p of prev. small ring, (3ds, p) 6 times, 3ds, cl, T, space.

R5: 5ds, j to 4th p of next 4th round medium ring, 5ds, cl, T, space.

R6 (small ring): 3ds, j to 7th p of prev. large ring, 3ds, cl, T, space.

* R7: 5ds, j to 4th p of next 4th round large ring, 5ds, cl, T, space.

R8 (small ring): 3ds, p, 3ds, cl, T, space.

R9: 5ds, j to 6th p of same 4th round large ring, 5ds, cl, T, space.

R10 (large ring): 3ds, j to p of prev. small ring, (3ds, p) 6 times, 3ds, cl, T, space.

R11: 5ds, j to 4th p of next 4th round medium ring, 5ds, cl, T, space.

R12 (small ring): 3ds, j to 7th p of prev. large ring, 3ds, cl, T, space.

Repeat from * 22 times, ending by joining to the base of R1. Cut and finish ends.

Composite mat set

These are called 'composite' mats because
the same motif is repeated several times to
make something larger and more
interesting than just one motif on its own.

Techniques: rings, chains, joins, reverse
work (turn), two shuttle tatting
Materials: 2 shuttles for motifs, 1 shuttle/1
ball for edging, size 20 thread
Measurements: small mat is 11cm (4¼in)
diameter; medium mat is 23cm (9in)
diameter; large mat is 37cm (14¾in)
diameter

Note: Shuttle designated holds *working
thread* for that ring or chain.

Motif: Each motif is made up of 12 'inner
rings' and 6 'outer rings'. The motif forms
an hexagon shape with the outer rings at
the corners of the hexagon [F].

(Shuttle 1)   R1 (inner ring): 3ds, p, 3ds, p,
              3ds, p, 3ds, cl, T.
(Shuttle 2)   Ch1: 8ds, T.
(Shuttle 1)   R2 (inner ring): 3ds, j to last p
              of prev. R, 3ds, p, 3ds, p,
              3ds, cl.
(Shuttle 1)   Ch2: 6ds, p, 5ds, T.
(Shuttle 2)   R3 (outer ring): 4ds, p, 3ds, p,
              4ds, cl, T.
(Shuttle 1)   Ch3: 5ds, j to p of prev. Ch, 6ds.
(Shuttle 1) * R4 (inner ring): 3ds, j to last p
              of prev. inner ring, 3ds, p,
              3ds, p, 3ds, cl, T.

18   Composite mat set

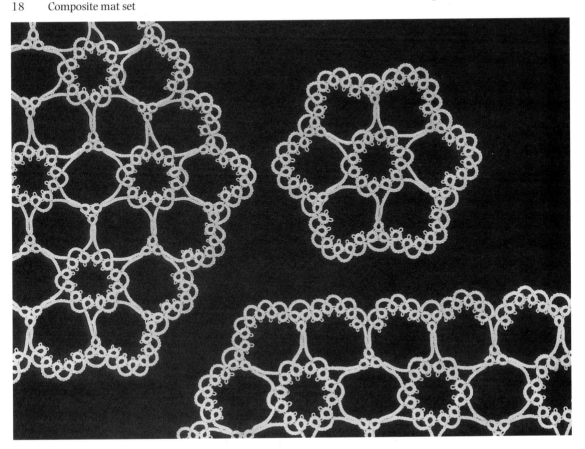

(Shuttle 2)   Ch4: 8ds, T.
(Shuttle 1)   R5 (inner ring): 3ds, j to last p
                of prev. R, 3ds, p, 3ds, p,
                3ds, cl.
(Shuttle 1)   Ch5: 6ds, p, 5ds, T.
(Shuttle 2)   R6 (outer ring): 4ds, p, 3ds, p,
                4ds, cl, T.
(Shuttle 1)   Ch6: 5ds, j to p of prev. Ch, 6ds.

Repeat from * 4 times, ending by joining to
base of R1. Cut and finish ends.

Small mat: Make 1 motif.
Medium mat: Make 7 motifs, joining *outer
rings* [G].
Large mat: Make 19 motifs, joining *outer
rings* [G].

The edging for these mats is made with 1
shuttle and 1 ball. One way of looking at this
edging is to distinguish between a 'corner'

F

G

H   corner section of edging

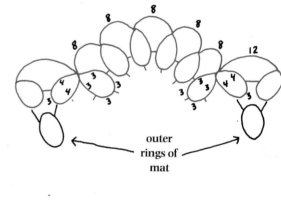

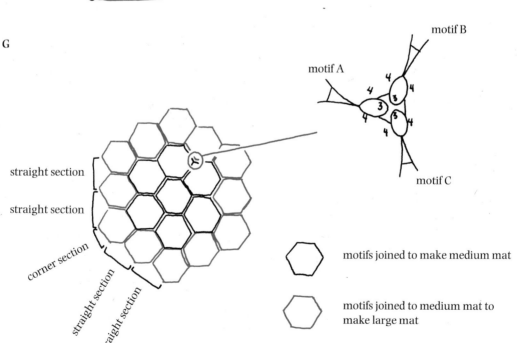

motif B

motif A

motif C

straight section

straight section

corner section

straight section

straight section

motifs joined to make medium mat

motifs joined to medium mat to
make large mat

I   **straight section of edging**

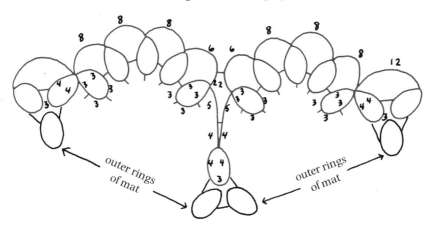

section [H] and a 'straight' section [I]. These sections are repeated and/or alternated around each mat as follows:

Small mat: Complete one corner section then repeat the corner section 5 times to complete edging.

Medium mat: Complete one corner section and one straight section, then repeat corner section/straight section 5 times to complete edging.

Large mat: Complete one corner section and *two* straight sections, then repeat corner section/straight section/straight section 5 times to complete edging.

Netted mat

Techniques: rings, chains, joins, reverse work (turn), netting (including measured spaces)

Materials: 1 shuttle, 1 ball, 6mm ($\frac{1}{4}$in) spacer, 1cm ($\frac{3}{8}$in) spacer, 1.3cm ($\frac{1}{2}$in) spacer, size 20 thread

Measurements: 22.5cm ($8\frac{3}{4}$in) × 16cm ($6\frac{1}{2}$in)

Note: All joins in centre strip, round one, round two, and round three are made using the *anchor* thread.

Centre strip

* R1: 6ds, p, 6ds, cl, T.
  Ch1: 4ds, p, 4ds, j to p of prev. R, T.

Repeat from * 9 times, but DO NOT TURN AFTER LAST CHAIN.

Ch11: 4ds, p, 4ds, j to small space between R9 and R10,
      4ds, p, 4ds, j to small space between R8 and R9,
      4ds, p, 4ds, j to small space between R7 and R8,
      4ds, p, 4ds, j to small space between R6 and R7,
      4ds, p, 4ds, j to small space between R5 and R6,
      4ds, p, 4ds, j to small space between R4 and R5,
      4ds, p, 4ds, j to small space between R3 and R4,
      4ds, p, 4ds, j to small space between R2 and R3,
      4ds, p, 4ds, j to small space between R1 and R2,
      4ds, p, 4ds, j to base of R1. Cut and finish ends.

1st round

Begin by joining to p of Ch1 of centre strip.
* Ch: (2ds, p) 3 times, 2ds, j to p of next Ch of centre strip.

Repeat from * 8 times, DO NOT BREAK THREAD.

Continue Ch: (2ds, p) 7 times, 2ds, j to p of next Ch of centre strip.

Repeat from * once, ending by joining to the same p as the very first join of this round. Cut and finish ends.

2nd round

Begin by joining to centre p of first Ch made in 1st round.

* Ch: 3ds, p, 2ds, p, 2ds, p, 3ds, j to centre p of next Ch in 1st round.

Repeat from * 7 times, DO NOT BREAK THREAD.

Continue Ch: 3ds, p, 2ds, p, 2ds, p, 3ds, j to *first* p of next Ch of 1st round, 3ds, p, 2ds, p, 2ds, p, 3ds, j to 4th p of same Ch of 1st round, 3ds, p, 2ds, p, 2ds, p, 3ds, j to 7th p of same Ch of 1st round, 3ds, p, 2ds, p, 2ds, p, 3ds, j to centre p of next Ch of 1st round, DO NOT BREAK THREAD.

Repeat from * *once*, ending by joining to the same p as the first join of this round. Cut and finish ends.

3rd round

Begin by joining to centre p of first Ch made in 2nd round.
* Ch: 3ds, p, 2ds, p, 2ds, p, 3ds, j to centre p of next Ch of 2nd round.

Repeat from * 7 times, DO NOT BREAK THREAD.

Ch: (2ds, p) 5 times, j to centre p of next Ch of 2nd round, (2ds, p) 5 times, j to centre p of next Ch of 2nd round, (2ds, p) 5 time, j to centre p of next Ch of 2nd round, 3ds, p, 2ds, p, 2ds, p, 3ds, j to centre p of next Ch of 2nd round, DO NOT BREAK THREAD.

Repeat from * *once*, ending by joining to the same p as the first join of this round. Cut and finish ends.

Netting: 1 shuttle

The diagram helps to make clear where the netting begins and the direction it takes.

Note: All rings are [3ds, j, 3ds, cl] unless otherwise stated.

Small space is 6mm ($\frac{1}{4}$in)
Medium space is 1cm ($\frac{3}{8}$in)
Large space is 13mm ($\frac{1}{2}$in)

1st round

See diagram J for placement of the 36 rings of this round. Note that some spaces are small (S) and some are medium (M). End

this round by joining the last space to the base of the first ring. DO NOT BREAK THREAD.

2nd round

Med space, R joined to first space of 1st round,
* Large space, R joined to next space of 1st round, repeat from * 7 times,
☐ Med space, R joined to next space of 1st round, repeat from ☐ 10 times,
● Large space, R joined to next space of 1st round, repeat from ● 6 times,
+ Med space, R joined to next space of 1st round, repeat from + 8 times. DO NOT BREAK THREAD.

3rd round

Med space, R joined to first space of 2nd round,
Med space, R joined to next space of 2nd round,

J

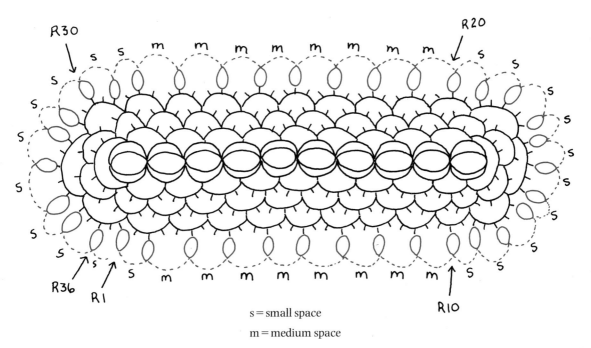

s = small space

m = medium space

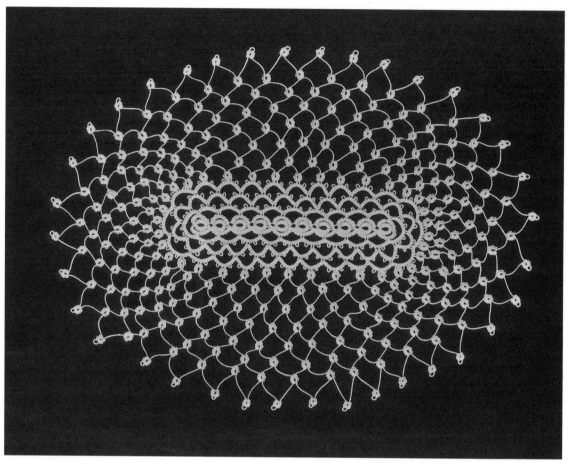

19   Netted mat

* Large space, R joined to next space of 2nd
round, repeat from * 7 times,
□ Med space, R joined to next space of 2nd
round, repeat from □ 9 times,
● Large space, R joined to next space of 2nd
round, repeat from ● 7 times,
+ Med space, R joined to next space of 2nd
round, repeat from + 7 times. DO NOT BREAK
THREAD.

4th round
Med space, R joined to first space of 3rd
round,
Med space, R joined to next space of 3rd
round,

* Large space, R joined to next space of 3rd
round, repeat from * 7 times,
□ Med space, R joined to next space of 3rd
round, repeat from □ 10 times,
● Large space, R joined to next space of 3rd
round, repeat from ● 6 times,
+ Med space, R joined to next space of 3rd
round, repeat from + 7 times. DO NOT BREAK
THREAD.

5th round
Med space, R joined to first space of 4th
round,
Med space, R joined to next space of 4th
round,

Med space, R joined to next space of 4th round,

* Large space, R joined to next space of 4th round, repeat from * 7 times,
☐ Med space, R joined to next space of 4th round, repeat from ☐ 10 times,
● Large space, R joined to next space of 4th round, repeat from ● 7 times,
+ Med space, R joined to next space of 4th round, repeat from + 5 times. DO NOT BREAK THREAD.

6th round
Med space, R joined to first space of 5th round,

Med space, R joined to next space of 5th round,

* Large space, R joined to next space of 5th round, repeat from * 33 times. DO NOT BREAK THREAD.

7th round
Large space, R joined to first space of 6th round,

Large space, R joined to next space of 6th round,

Med space, R joined to next space of 6th round, T,

* Med space, R of [3ds, p, 3ds, cl], T,
Med space, R joined to next space of 6th round, T, repeat from * 32 times,
Med space, R of [3ds, p, 3ds, cl], T,
Med space, R joined to first space of 7th round, T,
Med space, R of [3ds, p, 3ds, cl], T,
Med space, R joined to next space of 7th round, T,
Med space, R of [3ds, p, 3ds, cl], T,
Med space, R joined to next space of 7th round. Cut and finish ends.

Seven motif mat

Techniques: rings, chains, joins, large picot, reverse work (turn), two shuttle tatting
Materials: 2 shuttles, size 40 thread
Measurements: 13cm (5¼in) diameter

Note: Shuttle designated holds the *working thread* of that ring or chain.

First motif

(Shuttle 1)	R1: (2ds, p) 6 times, 2ds, cl, T.
(Shuttle 2)	Ch1: 2ds, p, 2ds, p, 2ds.
(Shuttle 2)	R2: 8ds, p, 8ds, cl, T.
(Shuttle 1)	Ch2: (2ds, p) 4 times, 2ds, j to p of prev. R using anchor thread, (2ds, p) 4 times, 2ds, T.
(Shuttle 2)	R3: 6ds, Lp, 6ds, cl, T.
(Shuttle 1)	Ch3: 3ds, p, 3ds, p, 3ds, p, 6ds, T.

20   Seven motif mat

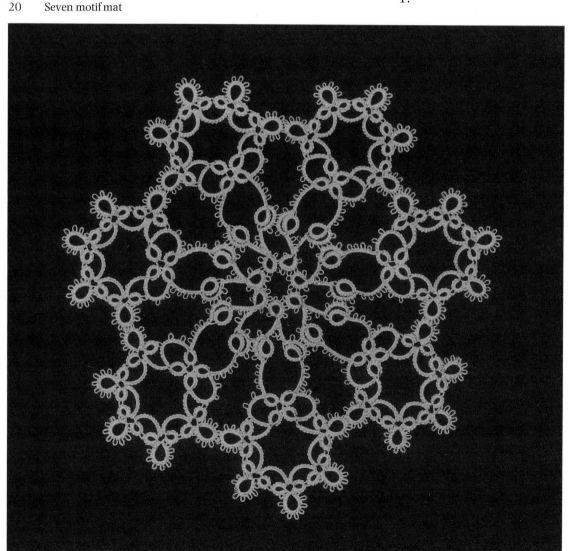

(Shuttle 2) R4: 6ds, j to Lp, 6ds, cl.

(Shuttle 2) Ch4: 8ds, T.

(Shuttle 1) *Clover* R5: 5ds, j to 3rd p of Ch3, 3ds, p, 2ds, cl.

R6: 2ds, j to last p of prev. R, (3ds, p) 8 times, 2ds, cl.

R7: 2ds, j to last p of prev. R, 3ds, p, 5ds, cl, T.

(Shuttle 2) * Ch5: 12ds, T.

(Shuttle 1) *Clover* R8: 5ds, j to last p of prev. R, 3ds, p, 2ds, cl.

R9: 2ds, j to last p of prev. R, (3ds, p) 8 times, 2ds, cl.

R10: 2ds, j to last p of prev. R, 3ds, p, 5ds, cl, T.

Repeat from * 3 times to complete 5 clovers.

(Shuttle 2) Ch9: 8ds

(Shuttle 2) R20: 6ds, j to Lp, 6ds, cl, T.

(Shuttle 1) Ch10: 6ds, j to last p of prev. clover, 3ds, p, 3ds, p, 3ds, T.

(Shuttle 2) R21: 6ds, j to Lp, 6ds, cl, T.

(Shuttle 1) Ch11: (2ds, p) 4 times, 2ds, T.

(Shuttle 2) R22: 8ds, p, 8ds, cl, T.

(Shuttle 1) Ch12: (2ds, p) 4 times, 2ds, j to p of prev. R using anchor thread, T.

(Shuttle 2) Ch13: 2ds, p, 2ds, j to 1st p of Ch1, 2ds, j to base of R1. Cut and finish ends.

Note that the two shuttle threads are shown as different colours for clarity.

Make seven motifs, joining them to adjacent motifs in *eight* places [K]:

5th p of R1
2nd and 3rd picots of Ch2
4th p of R6 (large ring of 1st clover)
6th p of R18 (large ring of last clover)
2nd and 3rd picots of Ch12
2nd p of R1.

K

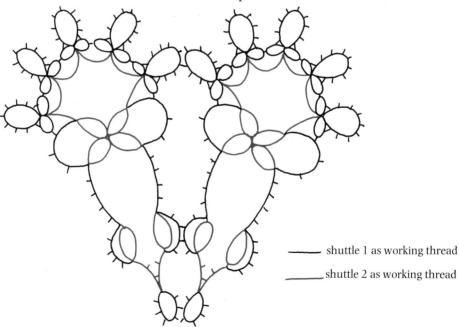

——— shuttle 1 as working thread

——— shuttle 2 as working thread

Collars

Two piece collar

Techniques: rings, chains, joins, reverse work (turn)
Materials: 1 shuttle, 1 ball, size 40 thread
Measurements: approx 5cm (2in) wide at front and 2.5cm (1in) at back.

1st round begins at back of neck:
R1: 8ds, p, 8ds, cl.
R2: 8ds, p, 8ds, cl, T.
* Ch1: 4ds, p, (2ds, p) 4 times, 4ds, T.
R3: 8ds, j to p of prev. R, 8ds, cl.
R4: 8ds, p, 8ds, cl, T.

Repeat from * 22 times, ending with R48.

Ch24: 4ds, j to last p of prev. Ch, 4ds, T.
R49: 6ds, p, 6ds, cl, T.
Ch25: 4ds, T.
R50: 4ds, p, 4ds, cl.
R51: 10ds, p, 10ds, cl, T.
Ch26: 4ds, p, 2ds, p, 3ds, j to 3rd p of Ch23 (chain opposite), 3ds, p, 2ds, p, 4ds, T.
R52: 10ds, j to p of prev. R, 10ds, cl.
* R53: 10ds, p, 10ds, cl, T.
Ch27: 4ds, p, 2ds, p, 3ds, j to 3rd p of Ch opposite, 3ds, p, 2ds, p, 4ds, T.
R54: 10ds, j to p of prev. R, 10ds, cl.

Repeat from * 14 times to make a total of 82 rings and 41 chains in 1st round. Cut and finish ends.

2nd round begins at back of neck, proceeds along *inside* edge of collar, then along outside edge to finally end again at back of neck.
R1: 6ds, j to 1st joined p of 1st round (that is, the p that is already joining R2 and R3 of 1st round), 6ds, cl, T.

Ch1: (2ds, p) 5 times, 2ds, T.
* R2: 6ds, j to next joined p of 1st round, 6ds, cl, T.
Ch2: (2ds, p) 5 times, 2ds, T.

Repeat from * 20 times, ending with Ch22.

R23: 6ds, j to next joined p of 1st round, 6ds, cl, T.
Ch23: (2ds, p) 6 times, 2ds, T.
R24: 6ds, j to free p of next R on 1st round, 6ds, cl, T.
Ch24: (2ds, p) 9 times, 2ds, T.
R25: 4ds, j to next free p (R49) of 1st round, 4ds, cl, T.
Ch25: (2ds, p) 7 times, 2ds, j to next free p (R50) of 1st round using anchor thread, (2ds, p) 6 times, 2ds, T.
R26: 12ds, j to next joined p of 1st round, 12ds, cl, T.
Ch26: (2ds, p) 9 times, 2ds, T.
* R27: 12ds, j to next joined p of 1st round, 12ds, cl, T.
Ch27: (2ds, p) 8 times, 2ds, T.

Repeat from * 3 times.

* R31: 10ds, j to next joined p of 1st round, 10ds, cl, T.
Ch31: (2ds, p) 7 times, 2ds, T.

Repeat from * 3 times.

* R35: 8ds, j to next joined p of 1st round, 8ds, cl, T.
Ch35: (2ds, p)7 times, 2ds, T.

Repeat from * 3 times.

* R39: 6ds, j to next joined p of 1st round, 6ds, cl, T.

21   Two piece collar

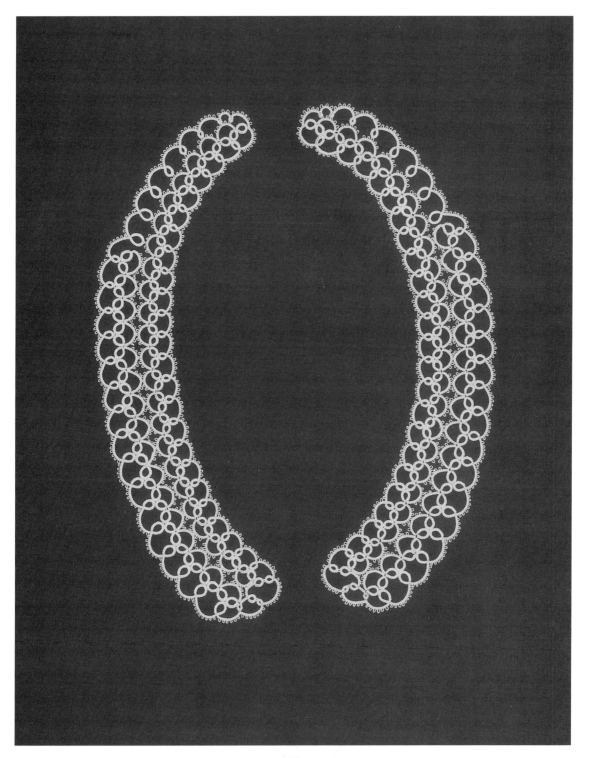

Ch39: (2ds, p) 7 times, 2ds, T.

Repeat from * once.

R41: 6ds, j to last joined p of 1st round, 6ds, cl, T.

Ch41: (2ds, p) 8 times, 2ds, T.

* R42: 12ds, j to 3rd p of next free Ch of 1st round, 12ds, cl, T.

Ch42: (2ds, p) 7 times, 2ds, T.

Repeat from * once.

R44: 10ds, j to 3rd p of next free Ch of 1st round, 10ds, cl, T.

Ch44: (2ds, p) 7 times, 2ds, T.

R45: 8ds, j to 3rd p of next free Ch of 1st round, 8ds, cl, T.

Ch45: (2ds, p) 7 times, 2ds, T.

R46: 6ds, j to 3rd p of next free Ch of 1st round, 6ds, cl, T.

Ch46: (2ds, p) 7 times, 2ds, T.

R47: 4ds, j to 3rd p of next free Ch of 1st round, 4ds, cl, T.

Ch47: (2ds, p) 6 times, 2ds, T.

R48: 2ds, j to 3rd p of last free Ch of 1st round, 2ds, cl, T.

Ch48: (2ds, p) 3 times, 2ds, T.

R49: 2ds, j to end p of same Ch of 1st round, 2ds, cl, T.

Ch49: (2ds, p) 6 times, 2ds, j to p of R1 of 1st round using anchor thread, (2ds, p) 7 times, 2ds, j to base of R1 of 2nd round. Cut and finish ends.

Repeat 1st and 2nd rounds to make the 2nd piece of the collar.

Collar in three rounds

Techniques: rings, chains, joins, reverse work (turn), large picots, half-closed rings

Materials: 1 shuttle, 1 ball, size 40 thread

Measurements: approx 4cm (1½in) wide. To fit a 38cm (15in) neckline.

1st round is a *ring only* round so only one shuttle is needed.

* R1: 2ds, p, 2ds, half-close.
R2: 2ds, p, 2ds, half-close.
R3 (centre ring): 3ds, p, 4ds, p, (2ds, p) 4 times, 3ds, cl, T, very small space.
R4: 5ds, p, 5ds, cl, j to last p of centre ring, very small space.
R5: 4ds, p, 2ds, p, 4ds, cl, j to 5th p of centre ring, very small space.
R6: 4ds, p, 2ds, p, 4ds, cl, j to 4th p of centre ring, very small space.
R7: 4ds, p, 2ds, p, 4ds, cl, j to 3rd p of centre ring, very small space.
R8: 5ds, p, 5ds, cl, j to 2nd p of centre ring, T, small space.
R9: 2ds, p, 2ds, half-close.
R10: 2ds, p, 2ds, half-close, small space.

Repeat from * 19 times. Cut and finish ends.

L

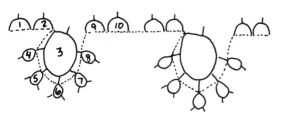

1st round: 1 repeat is 10 rings

2nd round is a motif repeated over and over. One shuttle and one ball are needed.

R1: 6ds, j to 2nd p of R7 in 1st round, 4ds, j to p of R8 in 1st round, 2ds, j to small space between R10 and R1 of 1st round, 2ds, j to p of next R4 of 1st round, 4ds, j to 1st p of R5 of 1st round, 6ds, cl, T.
Ch1: 2ds, T.
R2: 6ds, j to 2nd p of R5 of 1st round, 4ds, j to 1st p of R6 of 1st round, 4ds, p, 4ds, p, 6ds, cl, T.
Ch2: 2ds, T.
R3: 6ds, p, 4ds, p, 4ds, p, 4ds, p, 6ds, cl, T.
Ch3: 2ds, T.
R4: 6ds, p, 4ds, p, 4ds, j to 2nd p of R6 of 1st round, 4ds, j to 1st p of R7 of 1st round, 6ds, cl, T.
Ch4: 2ds, j to base of R1. Cut and finish ends.

Repeat this motif 18 times around collar.

M

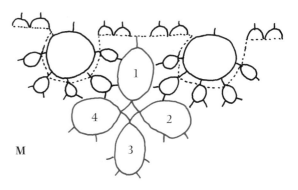

2nd round motif

3rd round is a *ring only* round so only one shuttle is needed.

Begin at one end of collar by joining thread to 1st p of the very first R5 in 1st round.

R(a): 4ds, p, (1ds, Lp) 14 times, 4ds, cl, small space, j to 2nd p of R5 in 1st round *and* to 1st p of R6 in 1st round.
R(b): 4ds, j to last p of prev. R, (1ds, Lp) 14 times, 4ds, cl, T.

R(c): 7ds, j to 2nd p of R4 of 2nd round motif, 3ds, cl, T, small space.

R(d): 2ds, j to last p of R(b), 3ds, p, 2ds, cl, T, small space.

R(e): 4ds, j to 1st p of R4 of 2nd round motif, 2ds, j to 4th p of R3 of 2nd round motif, 4ds, cl, T, small space.

R(f) (large R): 4ds, j to 2nd p of R(d), (1ds, Lp), 14 times, 4ds, cl, T, small space.

R5: 3ds, j to 3rd p of R3 of 2nd round motif, 3ds, cl, T, small space.

R6 (large R): 4ds, j to last p of prev. large ring, (1ds, Lp) 14 times, 4ds, cl, T, small space.

R7: 3ds, j to 2nd p of R3 of 2nd round motif, 3ds, cl, T, small space.

R8 (large R): 4ds, j to last p of R6, (1ds, Lp) 14 times, 4ds, cl, T, small space.

R9: 4ds, j to 1st p of R3 of 2nd round motif, 2ds, j to 4th p of R2 of 2nd round motif, 4ds, cl, T, small space.

22   Collar in three rounds (outside collar is a recently tatted version of the pattern; inside collar is a 1930s version of the pattern)

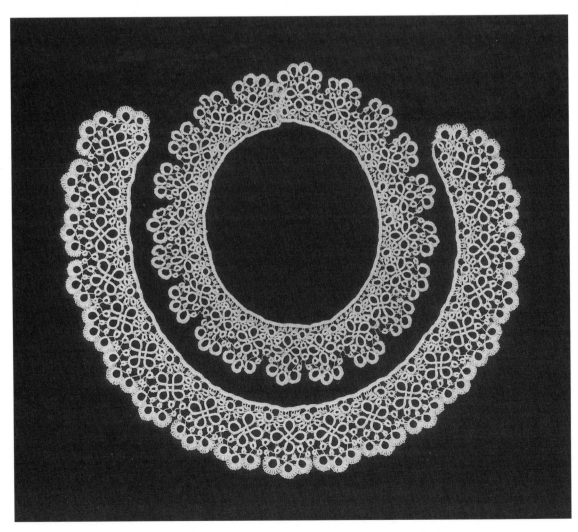

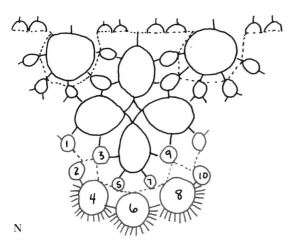

N

3rd round: 1 repeat is 10 rings

R10: 2ds, j to last p of R8, 5ds, cl, T, small space.
R1: 3ds, j to 3rd p of R2 of 2nd round motif, 4ds, j to 2nd p of R4 of 2nd round motif, 3ds, cl, T, small space.
R2: 5ds, p, 2ds, cl, T, small space.
R3: 4ds, j to 1st p of R4 of 2nd round motif, 2ds, j to 4th p of R3 of 2nd round motif, 4ds, cl, T, small space.
R4 (large R): 4ds, j to p of R2, (1ds, Lp) 14 times, 4ds, cl, T, small space.

Repeat from R5 17 times.

Repeat R5 through R9 once.

R(g): 2ds, j to last p of prev. large R, 3ds, p, 2ds, cl, T, small space.
R(h): 3ds, j to 3rd p of R2 of 2nd round motif, 7ds, cl, T, small space.
R(i): 4ds, j to last p of R(g), (1ds, Lp) 14 times, 4ds, cl, j to 2nd p of R6 of 1st round *and* 1st p of R7 of 1st round, small space.
R(j): 4ds, j to last p of prev. R, (1ds, Lp) 14 times, 4ds, cl, j to 2nd p of R7 of 1st round. Cut and finish ends.

Neck edge is finished in double crochet. The crochet edge is joined to each R1, R2, R3, R9, and R10 of 1st round. The curve of the collar may be adjusted by varying the number of double crochet stitches between joins.

This collar was made with 2 double crochet between R1 and R2 and between R9 and R10, 4 double crochet between R2 and R3 and between R3 and R9, and 3 double crochet between R10 and R1.

Round collar with twisted picots

Techniques: rings, chains, joins (including joining into a previously made join), twisted picots, measured picots

Materials: 1 shuttle, 1 ball, 2.5cm (1in) spacer, size 20 thread

Measurements: 6cm (2¼in) wide. To fit a 38cm (15in) neckline.

Note: To make a 13mm (½in) picot, measure a space of 2.5cm (1in) using a piece of card.

1st motif

Centre ring: 1ds, [13mm (½in) picot, 1ds] 8 times, cl. Cut and finish ends.

1st round

Note: Before joining to picots of centre ring, twist the picot approx 3 times.

R1: 5ds, j to any twisted p of centre ring, 5ds, cl, T.

* Ch1: 12ds, T.

R2: 5ds, j to next twisted p of centre ring, 5ds, cl, T.

Repeat from * 6 times, ending with R8.

Ch8: 12ds, j to base of R1. Cut and finish ends.

2nd round

To begin, j thread to small space between any two chains of 1st round.

23　Round collar with twisted picots

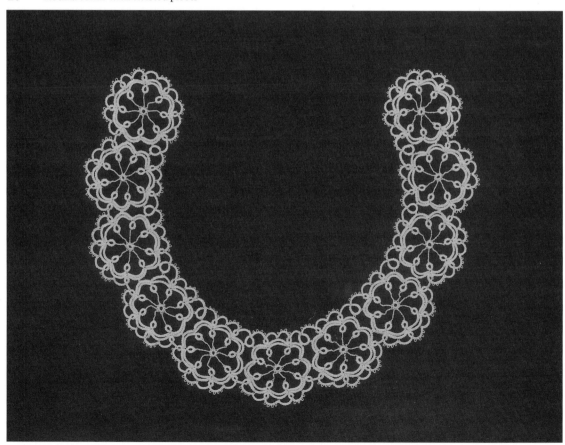

Ch1: * 7ds, p, 7ds, j to small space between next two chains of 1st round using anchor thread.

Repeat from * 7 times, joining last chain section to 1st chain section. Cut and finish ends.

2nd motif
Centre ring: Same as for 1st motif.
1st round: Same as for 1st motif.
2nd round: Same as for 1st motif, except j the 1st chain of 2nd motif to any chain (any free p) of 1st motif.

3rd motif and all subsequent motifs
Centre ring and 1st round: As for 1st motif.
2nd round: As for 1st motif, except j 1st chain of current motif to the 5th chain (4th free p) of previous motif.

Continue until 11 motifs are completed. This forms 1st round of the collar.

2nd round begins at back of neck on *outside* edge, works along outside edge, around the end motif, along the inside edge, around the final end motif, and finishes at the beginning.

Outside edge
R1: 4ds, j into prev. made join between Ch5 and Ch6 of end motif of 1st round, 4ds, cl, T.
** Ch1: 3ds, T.
R2: 4ds, j into prev. made join between Ch8 and Ch1 of next motif of 1st round, 4ds, cl, T.
* Ch2: (2ds, p) 4 times, 2ds, j to next free p of 1st round using anchor thread, 8ds, T.
R3: 4ds, j into next prev. made join between two chains of 1st round, 4ds, cl, T.

Repeat from * 2 times. This completes outside edge of one motif.

Repeat from ** 8 times. This completes outside edge of all but the end motifs. DO NOT BREAK THREADS.

Edge on 1st end motif
Ch1: 3ds, T.
R1: 4ds, j into prev. made join between Ch8 and Ch1 of next motif (end motif) of 1st round, 4ds, cl, T.
* Ch2: (2ds, p) 4 times, j to next free p of 1st round using anchor thread, 8ds, T.
R2: 4ds, j into next prev. made join between two chains of 1st round, 4ds, cl, T.

Repeat from * 5 times. DO NOT BREAK THREADS.

Inside edge
* Ch1: (2ds, p) 4 times, T.
R1: 7ds, j to last free p of end motif of 1st round, 5ds, j to 1st available free p of next motif of 1st round, 7ds, cl, T.
Ch2: 8ds, T.
R2: 4ds, j into next prev. made join between two chains of 1st round, 4ds, cl, T.
Ch3: (2ds, p) 4 times, j to next free p of 1st round using anchor thread, 8ds, T.
R3: 4ds, j into next prev. made join between two chains of 1st round, 4ds, cl, T.

Repeat from * 9 times. DO NOT BREAK THREAD.

Edge on final end
* Ch1: (2ds, p) 4 times, j to next free p of 1st round using anchor thread, 8ds, T.
R1: 4ds, j into next prev. made join between two chains of 1st round, 4ds, cl, T.

Repeat from * 3 times.

Final Ch: (2ds, p) 4 times, j to last free p of 1st round using anchor thread, 8ds, j to base of 1st ring of 2nd round. Cut and finish ends.

Square collar

Techniques: rings, chains, joins, josephine
  knots, two shuttle tatting
Materials: 1 shuttle/1 ball for motifs, 2
  shuttles for edging, size 40 thread
Measurements: Each motif is 2.5cm (1in) in
  diameter. Collar measures 24cm (9½in)
  wide × 25.5cm (10in) deep. Neck
  opening is 14cm (5½in) wide × 16.5cm
  (6½in) deep.

This composite design is based on a very
simple motif. The motifs can be joined to
make placemats or a tablecloth, but here
they are used to make a collar to fit a
pinafore yoke, with a dainty josephine knot
edging.

1st motif

Ring: (4ds, p) 5 times, 4ds, cl, T.
Chain: 9ds, p, 9ds, j to 1st p of ring using
  anchor thread, * 9ds, p, 9ds, j to next p
  of ring using anchor thread.

Repeat from * 4 times, making last j to the
base of the ring. Cut and finish ends.

Subsequent motifs

These are joined as shown in the
photograph to make squares or rectangles.
This collar, a pinafore yoke, is basically
three rectangles. Each strap is 7 motifs by 2
motifs, and the yoke section is a rectangle of
3 motifs by 9 motifs. If you are making a
glass mat, a square of 4 motifs by 4 motifs
would be a good size. A rectangle of 11
motifs by 14 motifs would be adequate for a
placemat.

Once all the motifs are joined into a basic
shape then an edging can be added. The
edging on the outside edge of the collar
would also be suitable on a placemat.

As you look at the collar, the motif in the top
right-hand corner will be considered the 1st
motif. The edging begins here and works
along the *outside* of the collar in a clockwise
direction.

Note: The outside edging requires 2 shuttle
tatting.
    All chains are made with shuttle 1 as
      working thread.
    All josephine knots are 10 half stitches
      made with shuttle 1.
    All rings are made with shuttle 2 as
      working thread.

Outside vertical edge

To begin, join thread to the 2nd free p of the
1st motif.
Ch1: 4ds, j.k., 4ds, j.k., 4ds, j to next free p of
  1st motif using anchor thread, 4ds, j.k.,
  4ds, j.k., 4ds, T.
R: 4ds, j to next p of 1st motif (it is already
  joined to next motif), 4ds, cl, T.
* Ch2: 4ds, j.k., 4ds, j.k., 4ds, j to next free p
  using anchor thread, 4ds, j.k., 4ds, j.k.,
  4ds, T.
R: 4ds, j to next p, 4ds, cl, T.

Repeat from * 7 times (or to length desired if
making a placemat). DO NOT BREAK THREAD.

Outside corner

Ch: * 4ds, j.k., 4ds, j.k., 4ds, j to next p using
  anchor thread.

Repeat from * twice. DO NOT BREAK THREAD.

Outside horizontal edge

Ch: * 4ds, j.k., 4ds, j.k., 4ds, j.k., 4ds, j to
  next free p using anchor thread, 4ds,
  j.k., 4ds, j.k., 4ds, j to next free p using
  anchor thread.

Repeat from * 7 times (or to length desired if
making a placemat). DO NOT BREAK THREAD.

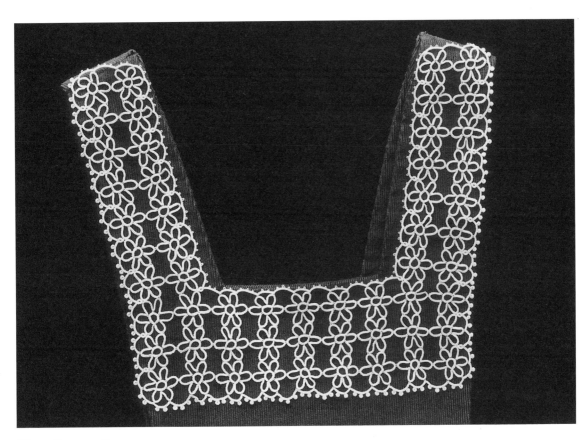

24   Square collar

Outside corner and second vertical edge

Ch: 4ds, j.k., 4ds, j.k., 4ds, j to next free p
    using anchor thread, 4ds, j.k., 4ds, j.k.,
    4ds, T.
* R: 4ds, j to next p (it is already joined to next
    motif), 4ds, cl, T.
Ch: 4ds, j.k., 4ds, j.k., 4ds, j to next free p
    using anchor thread, 4ds, j.k., 4ds, j.k.,
    4ds, T.

Repeat from * 8 times (or to length desired if
making a placemat) ending by joining the
final chain to the next free p using anchor
thread. (If you are putting the edging
around a placemat then you will need to
continue on with one more *outside horizontal
edge* to end up back at the starting point.)

1st inside vertical edge

Ch: 4ds, p, 4ds, p, 4ds, j to next free p using
    anchor thread, 4ds, p, 4ds, p, 4ds, p,
    4ds, j to next free p using anchor thread,
    4ds, p, 4ds, p, 4ds, j to next free p using
    anchor thread, 4ds, p, 4ds, p, 4ds j to
    next free p using anchor thread, 4ds, p,
    4ds, p, 4ds, T.
R: 4ds, j to next p (it is already joined to next
    motif), 4ds, cl, T.
* Ch: 4ds, p, 4ds, p, 4ds, j to next free p using
    anchor thread, 4ds, p, 4ds, p, 4ds, T.
R: 4ds, j to next p, 4ds, cl, T.

Repeat from * 5 times. DO NOT BREAK THREAD.

Inside horizontal edge

Ch: 4ds, p, 4ds, p, 4ds, j to next free p using anchor thread, 4ds, p, 4ds, p, 4ds, j to next free p using anchor thread, * 4ds, p, 4ds, p, 4ds, p, 4ds, j to next free p using anchor thread, 4ds, p, 4ds, p, 4ds, j to next free p using anchor thread.

Repeat from * 3 times. DO NOT BREAK THREAD.

2nd inside vertical edge

Ch: 4ds, p, 4ds, p, 4ds, T.
R: 4ds, j to next p (it is already joined to next motif), 4ds, cl, T.

* Ch: 4ds, p, 4ds, p, 4ds, j to next free p using anchor thread, 4ds, p, 4ds, p, 4ds, T.
R: 4ds, j to next p, 4ds, cl, T.

Repeat from * 5 times.

* Ch: 4ds, p, 4ds, p, 4ds, j to next free p using anchor thread.

Repeat from * twice.

Ch: 4ds, p, 4ds, p, 4ds, p, 4ds, j to last free p using anchor thread, 4ds, p, 4ds, p, 4ds, j to same p as the very first chain of the edging. The pinafore should be completely edged. Cut and finish ends.

Three-dimensional patterns

Bookmark

Techniques: rings, chains, joins, reverse
work (turn)
Materials: 1 shuttle, 1 ball, size 40 thread
Measurements: triangle $8 \times 8 \times 11$cm
($3\frac{1}{4} \times 3\frac{1}{4} \times 4\frac{1}{4}$in)

1st side

All rings are: 4ds, p (or j), 5ds, p (or j), 4ds,
cl, T.
All long chains are: 6ds, p (or j), 6ds, p (or j),
6ds, T.
All short chains are: 6ds, T.

Follow picture, beginning with ring 1,
joining rings and chains where shown.

2nd side

Repeat 1st side, joining to 1st side at picots
indicated in diagram 0.

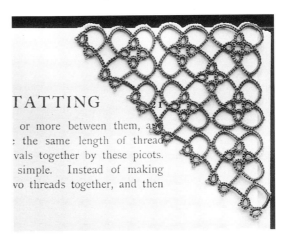

25   Bookmark

O

— join 2nd side at these picots

Baby Bootees

Techniques: rings, chains, joins, reverse
work (turn), large picots
Materials: 1 shuttle, 1 ball, size 20 thread
Measurements: sole is approx 7.5cm (3in)
long

Sole

R1: 6ds, Lp, 6ds, cl, T.
Ch1: (2ds, p) 6 times, 2ds, T.
R2: 6ds, j to Lp, 6ds, cl, T.
* Ch2: (2ds, p) 5 times, 2ds, T.
R3: 6ds, j to prev. Lp, 6ds, cl.
R4: 6ds, Lp, 6ds, cl, T.

Repeat from * 4 times.

Ch7: (2ds, p) 5 times, T.
R13: 6ds, j to prev. Lp, 6ds, cl, T.
Ch8: (2ds, p) 6 times, 2ds, T.
R14: 6ds, j to prev. Lp, 6ds, cl, T.
Ch9: (2ds, p) 5 times, 2ds, T.

P

sole

* R15: 6ds, j to same Lp as prev. R, 6ds, cl.
R16: 6ds, j to Lp opposite, 6ds, cl, T.
Ch10: (2ds, p) 5 times, 2ds, T.

Repeat from * 4 times, ending by joining last
chain to base of R1. Cut and finish ends.

1st round

R1: 6ds, j to any p of sole that is coloured in
diagram P, 6ds, cl.
R2: 6ds, j to next p of sole that is coloured in
diagram P, 6ds, cl, T.
Ch1: (2ds, p) 5 times, 2ds, T.

Q

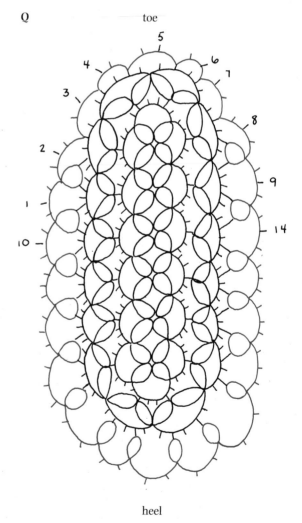

heel

* R3: 6ds, j to same p as prev. R, 6ds, cl.
R4: 6ds, j to next p of sole that is coloured in
diagram P, 6ds, cl, T.
Ch2: (2ds, p) 5 times, 2ds, T.

Repeat from * 14 times (all around sole),
ending by joining last chain to base of R1.
Cut and finish ends.

2nd round

See diagram Q, showing 2nd round in
coloured thread.

Rings with *one* join: 4ds, j, 4ds, cl, T.

Rings with *two* joins: 3ds, j, 3ds, j, 3ds, cl, T.

All chains have 2ds before and after each
picot. For number of picots in each chain see
diagram Q.

(*Note* that the chain lengths are distorted in
the diagram due to drawing a three-
dimensional object in two dimensions.) In
the toe section, the chains are joined to 1st
round picots using the anchor thread.

3rd round – toe motif

See diagram R for instructions on how to
make the toe motif. Begin with ring 'a',
indicated in diagram R, and proceed in a
clockwise direction.

All rings of the motif are the same: [6ds, p
(or j), 2ds, p (or j), 6ds, cl, T].

All chains have 2ds before and after each
picot (or join). Picots numbered 1 to 9 on
the toe motif are actually joins to 2nd
round. For example, picot no. 1 on the toe
motif is a join to picot no. 1 in 2nd round
(indicated in diagram Q).

Complete the toe motif, joining the final
chain to the base of ring 'a'. Cut and finish
ends.

R

toe motif

toe motif
edging

4th round – toe motif edging

See diagram R for instructions on how to
make the edging for the toe motif. Both rings
and chains have 2ds before and after each
picot (or join). Numbered picots are joined to
the corresponding picots of 2nd round and
the motif. Join no. 12 is made using anchor
thread. Cut and finish ends of edging.

5th round – bootee edging

Diagram S shows how the rings of the
bootee edging are joined to the picots of the
toe motif edging and to the remaining free
chains of 2nd round. Begin with ring 1,
indicated in diagram S.

R1: 6ds, j to toe edging, 3ds, Lp, 3ds, cl, T.
Ch1: 2ds, p, 2ds, p, 2ds, p, 2ds, T.
R2: 3ds, j to Lp of prev. R, 3ds, j to toe
edging, 3ds, Lp, 3ds, cl, T.
Ch2: 2ds, p, 2ds, p, 2ds, T.
R3: 3ds, j to Lp of prev. R, 3ds, j to heel, 3ds,
Lp, 3ds, cl, T.
* Ch3: 2ds, p, 2ds, p, 2ds, p, 2ds, T.
R4: 3ds, j to Lp of prev. R, 3ds, j to heel, 3ds,
Lp, 3ds, cl, T.

Repeat from * 9 times.

Ch13: 2ds, p, 2ds, p, 2ds, T.

R14: 3ds, j to Lp of prev. R, 3ds, j to toe
edging, 3ds, Lp, 3ds, cl, T.

Ch14: 2ds, p, 2ds, p, 2ds, p, 2ds, T.

R15: 3ds, j to Lp of prev. R, 3ds, j to toe
edging, 6ds, cl. Cut and finish ends.

Finishing

To shape bootee, saturate with spray starch
and finger-shape, then leave to dry. Weave a
6mm ($\frac{1}{8}$in) ribbon through the bootee edging
and tie in a bow at the front. Trim ribbon
edges.

S

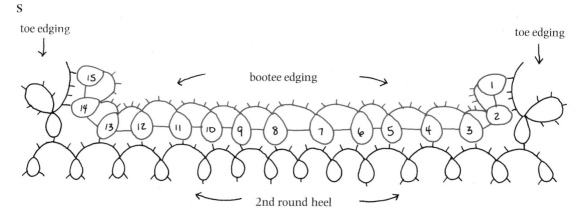

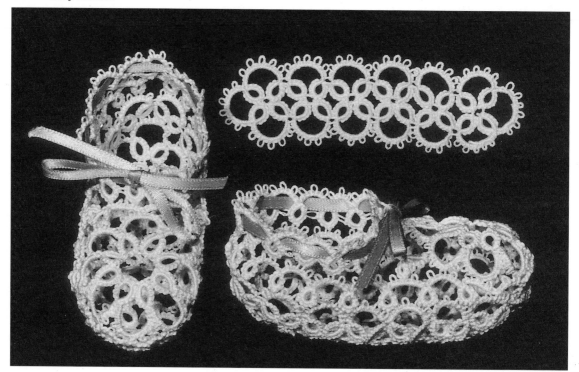

Small oval basket

Techniques: rings, chains, joins, reverse
work (turn), sets of stitches
Materials: 1 shuttle, 1 ball, size 40 thread,
20.5cm (8in) of 3mm ($\frac{1}{8}$in) ribbon
Measurements: base is 4 × 3.5cm
($1\frac{5}{8}$ × $1\frac{1}{4}$in); basket is approx. 2.5cm
(1in) high

Base

R1: (2ds, p) 7 times, 2ds, cl, T.
Ch1: (2ds, p) 5 times, 2ds, T.
R2: (2ds, p) 7 times, 2ds, cl, T.
Ch2: (2ds, p) 3 times, 1ds, T.
R3: (2ds, p) 7 times, 2ds, cl, T.
Ch3: 1ds, j to last p of prev. Ch, 2ds, p, 2ds,
p, 2ds, T.
R4: (2ds, p) 7 times, 2ds, cl, T.
Ch4: 2ds, p, 2ds, p, 2ds, j to centre p of Ch1,
2ds, p, 2ds, p, 2ds, T.
R5: (2ds, p) 7 times, 2ds, cl, T.
Ch5: (2ds, p) 3 times, 1ds, T.
R6: (2ds, p) 7 times, 2ds, cl, T.
Ch6: 1ds, j to last p of prev. Ch, 2ds, p, 2ds,
p, 2ds, j to base of R1.
Cut and finish ends.

T

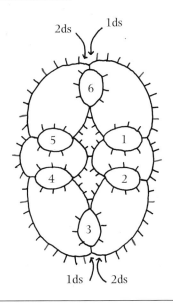

base   1ds   2ds

Chain around base

Look at diagram T and locate R1–R6. Join
thread to centre p of R6 and continue:
Ch: 1ds, p, (2ds, p) 9 times, 2ds, j to centre p
of R1 using anchor thread, (2ds, p) 5
times, 2ds, j to centre p of R2 using
anchor thread, (2ds, p) 9 times, 2ds, j to
centre p of R3 using anchor thread, 1ds,
p, (2ds, p) 9 times, 2ds, j to centre p of
R4 using anchor thread, (2ds, p) 5
times, 2ds, j to centre p of R5 using
anchor thread, (2ds, p) 9 times, 2ds, j to
centre p of R6 using anchor thread. Cut
and finish ends.

1st round of side

Look at diagram T and locate the coloured
picots. These are the picots to which 1st
round chains will be joined.

U

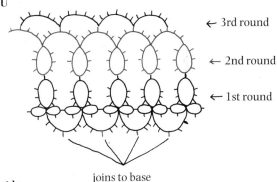

← 3rd round
← 2nd round
← 1st round

side   joins to base

Look at diagram U to see how the clovers are
joined to each other.

Clover: R1: (2ds, p) 3 times, 2ds, cl.
R2: 2ds, j to last p of R1, (2ds, p) 6
times, 2ds, cl.
R3: 2ds, j to last p of R2, 2ds, p, 2ds,
p, 2ds, cl, T.
Chain: 2ds, p, 2ds, p, 2ds, j to base, 2ds, p,
2ds, p, 2ds, T.

27   Small oval basket

2nd round of side

R1: (2ds, p) 3 times, 2ds, j to centre p of any
    clover of 1st round, (2ds, p) 3 times, 2ds,
    cl, T.
* Ch1: (2ds, p) 5 times, T.
R2: (2ds, p) 3 times, 2ds, j to centre p of next
    clover of 1st round, (2ds, p) 3 times, 2ds,
    cl, T.

Repeat from * 10 times.

Final Ch: (2ds, p) 5 times, j to base of R1. Cut
    and finish ends.

3rd round of side

Join thread to centre p of any Ch of 2nd
    round.
Ch: (2ds, p) 5 times, 2ds, j to centre p of next
    2nd round chain using anchor thread.

Repeat this chain all around. Cut and finish
ends.

Handle

Join thread to a 3rd round picot, wherever
you would like the handle to be attached.
Make sets of 3 until handle is approx. 6cm
(2¼in), then join the thread to a 3rd round
picot on the opposite side of the basket. Cut
and finish ends.

Finishing

To shape basket, saturate with spray starch
and finger-shape, then leave to dry. To
finish the basket, weave a 6mm (⅛in) ribbon
in and out of the spaces between 2nd and
3rd rounds. Tie ribbon in a bow and trim
ends.

Repeat clover and chain to make 12 clovers
and 12 chains. All clovers should be joined
as indicated in diagram of side and all
chains should be joined to base at picots
indicated in diagram of base. Join last Ch to
base of 1st clover. Cut and finish ends.

Small basket with brim

Techniques: rings, chains, large picots, joins
(including joining into a previously
made join), reverse work (turn), sets of
stitches

Materials: 1 shuttle, 1 ball, size 40 thread

Measurements: base is 4.5 × 3cm
($1\frac{3}{4}$ × $1\frac{1}{4}$in); basket is approx. 2.5cm
(1in) high

28   Small basket with brim

Base

R1: (2ds, p) 3 times, Lp, (2ds, p) 3 times,
    2ds, cl, T.

Ch1: (2ds, p) 10 times, 2ds, T.

Clover 1 R(a): (2ds, p) 3 times, cl.
      R(b): 2ds, j to last p of prev. R, 2ds,
        p, 2ds, p, 2ds, j to Lp of R1,
        (2ds, p) 3 times, 2ds, cl.
      R(c): 2ds, j to last p of prev. R, 2ds,
        p, 2ds, p, 2ds, cl, T.

Ch2: (2ds, p) 5 times, 2ds, T.

Clover 2 R(a): 2ds, p, 2ds, j to centre p of last
      R(c), 2ds, p, 2ds, cl.
      R(b): 2ds, j to last p of prev. R, (2ds,
        p) 6 times, 2ds, cl.
      R(c): 2ds, j to last p of prev. R, 2ds,
        p, 2ds, p, 2ds, cl, T.

Ch3: (2ds, p) 5 times, 2ds, T.

Clover 3 R(a): 2ds, p, 2ds, j to centre p of last
      R(c), 2ds, p, 2ds, cl.
      R(b): 2ds, j to last p of prev. R, 2ds,
        p, 2ds, p, 2ds, Lp, (2ds, p) 3
        times, 2ds, cl.
      R(c): 2ds, j to last p of prev. R, 2ds,
        p, 2ds, p, 2ds, cl, T.

Ch4: (2ds, p) 10 times, 2ds, T.

R2: (2ds, p) 2 times, 2ds, j to Lp of prev.
    clover, (2ds, p) 3 times, 2ds, cl, T.

Ch5: (2ds, p) 10 times, 2ds, T.

Clover 4 R(a): (2ds, p) 3 times, 2ds, cl.
      R(b): 2ds, j to last p of prev. R, 2ds,
        p, 2ds, p, 2ds, j to Lp of prev.
        clover, (2ds, p) 3 times, 2ds, cl.
      R(c): 2ds, j to last p of prev. R, 2ds,
        p, 2ds, p, 2ds, cl, T.

Ch6: (2ds, p) 5 times, 2ds, T.

Clover 5 R(a): 2ds, p, 2ds, j to centre p of last
      R(c), 2ds, p, 2ds, cl.
      R(b): 2ds, j to last p of prev. R, 2ds,
        p, 2ds, p, 2ds, j to centre p of
        clover opposite, (2ds, p) 3
        times, 2ds, cl.
      R(c): 2ds, j to last p of prev. R, 2ds,
        p, 2ds, p, 2ds, cl, T.

Ch7: (2ds, p) 5 times, 2ds, T.

Clover 6 R(a): 2ds, p, 2ds, j to centre p of last
R(c), 2ds, p, 2ds, cl.
R(b): 2ds, j to last p of prev. R, 2ds,
p, 2ds, p, 2ds, j to Lp of R1,
(2ds, p) 3 times, 2ds, cl.
R(c):2ds, j to last p of prev. R, 2ds,
p, 2ds, p, 2ds, cl, T.
Ch8: (2ds, p) 10 times, 2ds, j to base of R1.
Cut and finish ends.

1st round of side

Look at diagram V and locate the coloured
picots. These are the picots to which 1st
round chains will be joined, starting with
picot 1.

V

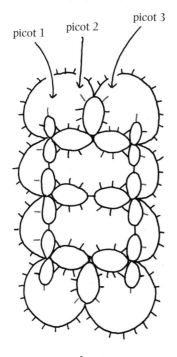

base

Look at diagram W for instructions on how
to complete 1st round. All rings are: [5ds, j
to base, 5ds, cl, T]. All chains have 2ds
before and after each picot. For number of
picots in each chain refer to diagram W.

Each ring is joined to the base as indicated:
the first ring made is joined to picot 1 of the
base, the second ring is joined to picot 2, and
so on, all around the base.

Join last chain to the base of the 1st ring.
Cut and finish ends.

2nd round of side

Look at the diagram W to see how 2nd
round clovers are joined to each other as
well as joined to 1st round chains.

All clovers: R(a): 2ds, p, 2ds, p (or j to prev.
clover), 2ds, p, 2ds, cl.
R(b): 2ds, j to last p of prev. R, 2ds,
p, 2ds, p, 2ds, j to 1st round,
2ds, p, 2ds, p, 2ds, p, 2ds, cl.
R(c): 2ds, j to last p of prev. R,
2ds, p, 2ds, p, 2ds, cl, T.

All chains: (2ds, p) 5 times, 2ds, T.

Make sure R(c) of the last clover is joined to
R(a) of the first clover.

Join the last chain to the base of the first
clover. Cut and finish ends.

Brim

Begin by joining thread to the centre p of
any 2nd round chain.

1st round: * 9ds, j to centre p of next 2nd
round chain using anchor thread, repeat
from * 13 times, making last j to the same p
as the first join of this round. DO NOT BREAK
THREAD.

2nd round: * 10ds, j into next prev. made
join using anchor thread, repeat from * 13
times. DO NOT BREAK THREAD.

3rd round: * 12ds, j into next prev. made
join using anchor thread, repeat from * 13
times. DO NOT BREAK THREAD.

W   side

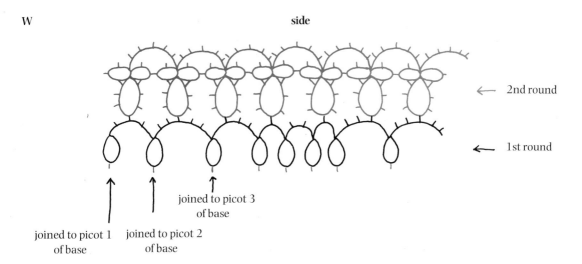

← 2nd round

← 1st round

joined to picot 3
of base

joined to picot 1   joined to picot 2
of base   of base

4th round: * (2ds, p) 7 times, 2ds, j into next prev. made j using anchor thread, repeat from * 13 times. Cut and finish ends.

Handle
Join thread to the centre p of a 2nd round chain (it will already be joined to the brim) wherever you would like the handle to be attached. Make 17 sets of 3 (or to length desired), then join thread to the centre p of the 2nd round chain on the opposite side of

the basket. Again, make 17 sets of 3. Twist this second handle around the first handle several times, then make a final join back at the beginning of the first handle. Cut and finish ends. A small dot of glue may be necessary at the beginning of the handle to secure the thread ends.

Finishing
To shape basket, saturate with spray starch and finger-shape, then leave to dry.

Christmas ball

Techniques: rings, netting (including measured spaces), joins

Materials: 1 shuttle, size 20 thread, 6mm ($\frac{1}{4}$in) spacer, 1cm ($\frac{3}{8}$in) spacer, 5cm (2in) diameter ball

Measurements: worked on a 5cm (2in) diameter Christmas ball

Bottom ring

1ds, p, (2ds, p) 15 times, 1ds, cl. Cut and finish ends. Set this ring aside till needed later.

Top ring

2ds, p, (3ds, p) 7 times, 1ds, cl. Cut and finish ends.

Netting

Note: All rings are [3ds, j, 3ds, cl].
Small space is 6mm ($\frac{1}{4}$in).
Medium space is 1cm ($\frac{3}{8}$in).
Extra large space is approx. 2–2.5cm ($\frac{3}{4}$–1in).

1st round: R joined to any p of top ring, * small space, R joined to next p of top ring.

Repeat from * 6 times, small space, j to base of 1st ring of this round. DO NOT BREAK THREAD.

2nd round: small space, R joined to first space of 1st round, * medium space, R joined to next space of 1st round.

29 Christmas ball: bottom view (*left*); side view (*middle*); top view (*right*)

Repeat from * 6 times. DO NOT BREAK THREAD.

3rd round: small space, R joined to first space of 2nd round, small space, R joined to same space as prev. R, * small space, R joined to next space of 2nd round, small space, R joined to same space as prev. R.

Repeat from * 6 times. DO NOT BREAK THREAD.

4th round: medium space, R joined to first space of 3rd round, * medium space, R joined to next space of 3rd round.

Repeat from * 14 times. DO NOT BREAK THREAD.

5th round: medium space, R joined to first space of 4th round, * medium space, R joined to next space of 4th round.

Repeat from * 14 times. DO NOT BREAK THREAD.

6th round: medium space, R joined to first space of 5th round,* medium space, R joined to next space of 5th round.

Repeat from * 14 times. DO NOT BREAK THREAD.

Position the netting over the top half of the Christmas ball. Position the bottom ring on the Christmas ball and continue:

Final round: extra large space, j to any p of bottom ring, extra large space, j to first space of 6th round, * extra large space, j to next p of bottom ring, extra large space, j to next space of 6th round.

Repeat from * until all picots of the bottom ring have been joined. The final join will be to the last space of 6th round. Secure thread with a knot. Cut thread. Dab a small amount of glue onto the final join to secure it.

Bibliography

Attenborough, Bessie, *The Craft of Tatting*, Bell & Hyman, 1985.

Jones, Rebecca, *The Complete Book of Tatting*, Dryad Press/Batsford/Kangaroo Press, 1985.

Konior, Mary, *A Pattern Book of Tatting*, Dryad Press/Batsford, 1985

Konior, Mary, *Tatting in Lace*, Dryad Press/Batsford, 1988.

Konior, Mary, *Tatting Patterns*, B.T. Batsford, 1989.

Orr, Anne, *Classic Tatting Patterns*, Dover, 1985.

Sanders, Julia, *Tatting Patterns*, Dover, 1977.

Weiss, Rita, *Tatting Doilies & Edgings*, Dover, 1980.

Weiss, Rita, *Traditional Tatting Patterns*, Dover, 1986.

Festive Tatting (DMC No. 15218), DMC, 1983.

Learn Tatting (Coats No. 1088), J & P Coats, 1987.

Learn to Tat (Anchor No. 17761), Lyric Books, 1990.

Tatting (DMC No. 8632), DMC, 1987.

Tatting for Today (DMC No. 15209), DMC, 1980.

Book suppliers

ENGLAND

The following are stockists of the complete Batsford/Dryad Press range:

Avon
Bridge Bookshop
7 Bridge Street
Bath BA2 4AS

Waterstone & Co.
4–5 Milsom Street
Bath BA1 1DA

Bedfordshire
Arthur Sells
Lane Cove
49 Pedley Lane
Clifton
Shefford SG17 5QT

Berkshire
Loricraft
4 Big Lane
Lambourn

West End Lace Supplies
Ravensworth Court Road
Mortimer West End
Reading RG7 3UD

Buckinghamshire
J. S. Sear Lacecraft Supplies
8 Hillview
Sheringham MK16 9NY

Cambridgeshire
Dillons the Bookstore
Sidney Street
Cambridge

Cheshire
Lynn Turner
Church Meadow Crafts
7 Woodford Rd
Winsford

Cornwall
Creative Books
22A River Street
Truro TR1 2SJ

Devon
Creative Crafts &
    Needlework
18 High Street
Totnes TQ9 5NP

Honiton Lace Shop
44 High Street
Honiton EX14 8PJ

Dorset
F. Herring & Sons
High Street West
Dorchester DT1 1UP

Tim Parker (mail order)
124 Corhampton Road
Boscombe East
Bournemouth BH6 5NL

Christopher Williams
19 Morrison Avenue
Parkstone
Poole BH17 4AD

Durham
Lacemaid
6, 10 & 15 Stoneybeck
Bishop Middleham
DL17 9BL

Gloucestershire
Southgate Handicrafts
63 Southgate Street
Gloucester GL1 1TX

Waterstone & Company
89–90 The Promenade
Cheltenham GL50 1NB

Hampshire
Creative Crafts
11 The Square
Winchester SO23 9ES

Doreen Gill
14 Barnfield Road
Petersfield GU31 4DR

Larkfield Crafts
4 Island Cottages
Mapledurwell
Basingstoke RG23 2LU

Needlestyle
24–26 West Street
Alresford

Ruskins
27 Bell Street
Romsey

Isle of Wight
Busy Bobbins
Unit 7
Scarrots Lane
Newport PO30 1JD

Kent
The Handicraft Shop
47 Northgate
Canterbury CT1 1BE

Hatchards
The Great Hall
Mount Pleasant Road
Tunbridge Wells

London
W. & G. Foyle Ltd
113–119 Charing Cross
Road WC2H 0EB

Hatchards
187 Piccadilly W1V 9DA

Middlesex
Redburn Crafts
Squires Garden Centre
Halliford Road
Upper Halliford
Shepperton TW17 8RU

Norfolk
Alby Lace Museum
Cromer Road
Alby
Norwich NR11 7QE

Jane's Pincushions
Taverham Craft Unit 4
Taverham Nursery Centre
Fir Covert Road
Taverham
Norwich NR8 6HT

Waterstone & Co.
30 London Street
Norwich NR2 1LD

Northamptonshire
Denis Hornsby
149 High Street
Burton Latimer
Kettering NN15 5RL

Somerset
Bridge Bookshop
62 Bridge Street
Taunton TA1 1UD

Staffordshire
J. & J. Ford
October Hill
65 Upper Way
Upper Longdon
Rugeley WS16 1QB

Sussex
Waterstone & Company Ltd
120 Terminus Road
Eastbourne

Warwickshire
Christine & David Springett
21 Hillmorton Road
Rugby CV22 6DF

Wiltshire
Everyman Bookshop
5 Bridge Street
Salisbury SP1 2ND

North Yorkshire
Craft Basics
9 Gillygate
York

Shireburn Lace
Finkel Court
Finkel Hill
Sherburn in Elmet LS25 6EB

The Craft House
23 Bar Street
Scarborough YO13 9QE

West Midlands
Needlewoman
Needles Alley
off New Street
Birmingham

West Yorkshire
Just Lace
14 Ashwood Gardens
Gildersome
Leeds LS27 7AS

Sebalace
Waterloo Mill
Howden Road
Silsden BD20 0HA

George White Lacemaking
Supplies
40 Heath Drive
Boston Spa LS23 6PB

Jo Firth
58 Kent Crescent
Lowtown, Pudsey
Leeds LS28 9EB

WALES

Bryncraft Bobbins (mail
order)
B. J. Phillips
Pantglas
Cellan
Lampeter
Dyfed SA48 BJD

Hilkar Lace Supplies
33 Mysydd Road
Landore
Swansea

SCOTLAND

Embroidery Shop
51 William Street
Edinburgh
Lothian EH3 7LW

Waterstone & Company
236 Union Street
Aberdeen AB1 1TN

Equipment suppliers

UNITED KINGDOM

General equipment

Alby Lace Museum
Cromer Road
Alby
Norwich
Norfolk NR11 7QE

Busy Bobbins
Unit 7
Scarrots Lane
Newport
IOW PO30 1JD

Chosen Crafts Centre
46 Winchcombe Street
Cheltenham
Glos GL52 2ND

Jo Firth
Lace Marketing &
    Needlecraft Supplies
58 Kent Crescent
Lowtown
Pudsey
W Yorks LS28 9EB

J. & J. Ford
October Hill
Upper Way
Upper Longdon
Rugeley
Staffs WS16 1QB

Framecraft
83 Hampstead Road
Handsworth Wood
Birmingham B2 1JA

R. Gravestock
Highwood
Crews Hill
Alfrick
Worcs WR6 5HP

The Handicraft Shop
47 Northgate
Canterbury
Kent CT1 1BE

Frank Herring & Sons
27 High West Street
Dorchester
Dorset DT1 1UP

Hilkar Lace Suppliers
33 Mysydd Rd
Landore
Swansea

Honiton Lace Shop
44 High Street
Honiton
Devon

Denis Hornsby
149 High Street
Burton Latimer
Kettering
Northants NN15 5RL
also at:
25 Manwood Avenue
Canterbury
Kent CT2 7AH

Frances Iles
73 High Street
Rochester
Kent ME1 1LX

Jane's Pincushions
Unit 4
Taverham Crafts
Taverham Nursery Centre
Fir Covert Road
Taverham
Norwich NR8 6HT

Just Lace
14 Ashwood Gardens
Gildersome
Leeds LS27 7AS

Loricraft
4 Big Lane
Lambourn
Berkshire

Needlestyle
5 The Woolmead
Farnham
Surrey GU9 7TX

Needlestyle
24–26 West Street
Alresford
Hants

Needlework
Ann Bartleet
Bucklers Farm
Coggeshall
Essex CO6 1SB

Needle and Thread
80 High Street
Horsell
Woking
Surrey GU21 4SZ

The Needlewoman
21 Needles Alley
off New Street
Birmingham B2 5AE

T. Parker
124 Corhampton Road
Boscombe East
Bournemouth
Dorset BH6 5NZ

Jane Playford
North Lodge
Church Close
West Runton
Norfolk NR27 9QY

Redburn Crafts
Squires Garden Centre
Halliford Road
Upper Halliford
Shepperton
Middx TW17 8RU

Christine Riley
53 Barclay Street
Stonehaven
Kincardineshire
Scotland

Peter & Beverley Scarlett
Strupak
Hill Head
Cold Wells, Ellon
Grampian
Scotland

Ken & Pat Schultz
134 Wisbech Road
Thornley
Peterborough

J. S. Sears
Lacecraft Supplies
8 Hillview
Sherington
Bucks MK16 9NY

Sebalace
Waterloo Mills
Howden Road
Silsden
W Yorkshire BD2 0NA

A. Sells
49 Pedley Lane
Clifton
Shefford
Beds

Shireburn Lace
Finkle Court
Finkle Hill
Sherburn in Elmet
N Yorks LS25 6EB

SMP
4 Garners Close
Chalfont St Peter
Bucks SL9 0HB

Southern Handicrafts
20 Kensington Gardens
Brighton
Sussex BN1 4AC

Spangles
Carole Morris
Cashburn Lane
Burwell
Cambs CB5 0ED

Stitchery
Finkle Street
Richmond
N. Yorks

Stitches
Dovehouse Shopping Parade
Warwick Road
Olton
Solihull
W Midlands

Teazle Embroideries
35 Boothferry Road
Hull
N Humberside

Lynn Turner
Church Meadow Crafts
7 Woodford Road
Winsford
Cheshire

The Craft House
23 Bar Street
Scarborough
N Yorks

George Walker
The Corner Shop
Rickinghall, Diss
Norfolk

West End Lace Supplies
Ravensworth Court Road
Mortimer West End
Reading
Berks RG7 3UD

George White Lacemakers'
    Supplies
40 Heath Drive
Boston Spa
W Yorks L23 6PB

Bobbins
A. R. Archer
The Poplars
Shetland
near Stowmarket
Suffolk IP14 3DE

Bartlett, Caesar and
    Partners
12 Creslow Court
Stony Stratford
Milton Keynes MK11 1NN
    also at:
The Glen
Shorefield Road
Downton
Lymington
Hants SO41 0LH

T. Brown
Temple Lane Cottage
Littledean
Cinderford
Glos

Bryncraft Bobbins
B. J. Phillips
Pantglas
Cellan
Lampeter
Dyfed SA48 BJD

Chrisken Bobbins
26 Cedar Drive
Kingsclere
Berks RG15 8TD

Malcolm J. Fielding
2 Northern Terrace
Moss Lane
Silverdale
Lancs LA5 0ST

Richard Gravestock
Highwood
Crews Hill
Alfrick
Worcs WR6 5HF

Larkfield Crafts
Hilary Ricketts
4 Island Cottages
Mapledurwell
Basingstoke
Hants RG25 2LU

Loricraft
4 Big Lane
Lambourn
Berks

T. Parker
124 Corhampton Road
Boscombe East
Bournemouth
Dorset BH6 5NZ

D. H. Shaw
47 Lamor Crescent
Thrushcroft
Rotherham
S Yorks S66 9QD

Christine & David Springett
21 Hillmorton Road
Rugby
War CV22 5DF

Richard Viney
Unit 7
Port Royal Street
Southsea
Hants PO5 3UD

West End Lace Suppliers
Ravensworth Court Road
Mortimer West End
Reading
Berks RG7 3UD

Winslow Bobbins
70 Magpie Way
Winslow
Bucks MK18 3PZ

Lace pillows
Newnham Lace Equipment
15 Marlowe Close
Basingstoke
Hants RG24 9DD

Bartlett, Caesar and
    Partners
12 Creslow Court
Stony Stratford
Milton Keynes MK11 1NN
    also at:
The Glen
Shorefield Road
Downton
Lymington
Hants SO41 0LH

**Silk embroidery and lace
    thread**
E. & J. Piper
Silverlea
Flax Lane
Glemsford
Suffolk CO10 7RS

Silk weaving yarn
Hilary Chetwynd
Kipping Cottage
Cheriton, Alresford
Hants SO24 0PW

Frames and mounts
Doreen Campbell
Highcliff
Bremilham Road
Malmesbury
Wilts SN16 0DQ

**Matt coloured transparent
    adhesive film**
Heffers Graphic Shop
26 King Street
Cambridge CB1 1LN

**Linen by the metre (yard)
    and made up articles of
    church linen**
Mary Collins
Church Furnishings
St Andrews Hall
Humber Doucy Lane
Ipswich
Suffolk IP4 3BP

Hayes & French
Head Office & Factory
Hanson Road
Aintree
Liverpool L9 9BP

Tatting equipment (shuttles, threads, and accessories)

W. J. and R. Ramsey
(*craftsman-made shuttles*)
11 Speke Close
Merriot
Crewkerne, Somerset

Coats Leisure Crafts
39 Durham Street
Glasgow G41 1BS

Gary Crafts (*craftsman-made shuttles*)
Invergarry
Inverness-shire
Scotland PH35 4HG

D. J. Hornsby
149 High Street
Burton Latimer
Kettering
Northants NN15 5RL

Sebalace
Waterloo Mill
Howden Road
Silsden
W. Yorks BD20 0AH

A. Sells
49 Pedley Lane
Clifton
Shefford, Beds

C. & D. Springett
21 Hamilton Road
Rugby
War. CV22 5DF

George White
40 Heath Drive
Boston Spa
W. Yorks L523 6PB

REPUBLIC OF IRELAND

Anne Keller (*craftsman-made shuttles*)
Coolvally
Abingdon Park
Shankill
Co. Dublin

UNITED STATES OF AMERICA

General equipment suppliers

Arbor House
22 Arbor Lane
Roslyn Hights
NY 11577

Baltazor Inc.
3262 Severn Avenue
Metairie
LA 7002

Beggars' Lace
P.O. Box 17263
Denver
Colo 80217

Berga Ullman Inc.
P.O. Box 918
North Adams
MA 01247

Frederick J. Fawcett
129 South Street
Boston
MA 02130

Frivolité
15526 Densmore N.
Seattle
WA 98113

Happy Hands
3007 S. W. Marshall
Pendleton
Oreg 97180

International Old Lacers
P.O. Box 1029
Westminster
Colo 80030

Lace Place de Belgique
800 S. W. 17th Street
Roca Raton
FL 33432

Lacis
2150 Stuart Street
Berkeley
CA 9470

Robin's Bobbins
RTL Box 1736
Mineral Bluff
GA 30559

Robin and Russ
Handweavers
533 North Adams Street
McMinnvills
Oreg 97128

Some Place
2990 Adline Street
Berkeley
CA 94703

Osma G. Todd Studio
319 Mendoza Avenue
Coral Gables
FL 33134

The Unique And Art Lace
  Cleaners
5926 Delman Boulevard
St Louis
MO 63112

Van Scriver Bobbin Lace
130 Cascadilla Park
Ithaca
NY 14850

The World in Stitches
82 South Street
Milford
N.H. 03055

Tatting equipment

Susan Bates
212 Middlesex Ave.
Chester
Ct. 06412

Lacis
2982 Adeline Street
Berkeley
Cal. 94703

The Stitchworks
6011 S. Sheridan Rd.
Tulsa
Oklahoma 74145

AUSTRALIA

General equipment suppliers

Australian Lace magazine
P.O. Box 1291
Toowong
Queensland 4066

Dentelles Lace Supplies
c/o Betty Franks
39 Lang Terrace
Northgate 4013
Brisbane
Queensland

The Lacemaker
94 Fordham Avenue
Hartwell
Victoria 3124

Spindle and Loom
Arcade 83
Longueville Road
Lane Cove
NSW 2066

Tulis Crafts
201 Avoca Street
Randwick
NSW 2031

BELGIUM

't Handwerkhuisje
Katelijnestraat 23
8000 Bruges

Kantcentrum
Balstraat 14
8000 Bruges

Manufacture Belge de
  Dentelle
6 Galerie de la Reine
Galeries Royales St Hubert
1000 Bruxelles

Orchidée
Mariastraat 18
8000 Bruges

Ann Thys
't Apostelientje
Balstraat 11
8000 Bruges

FRANCE

Centre d'Initiations à la
  Dentelle du Puy
2 Rue Duguesclin
43000 Le Puy en Velay

A L'Econome
Anne-Marie Deydier
Ecole de Dentelle aux
    Fuseaux
10 Rue Paul Chenavard
69001 Lyon

Rougier and Plé
13–15 bd des Filles de
    Calvaire
75003 Paris

WEST GERMANY

Der Fenster Laden
Berliner Str. 8
D 6483 Bad Soden
Salmünster

P.P. Hempel
Ortolanweg 34
1000 Berlin 47

Heikona De Ruijter
Klöppelgrosshandel
Langer Steinweg 38
D4933 Blomberg

HOLLAND

Blokker's Boektiek
Bronsteeweg 4/4a
2101 AC Heemstede

Theo Brejaart
Dordtselaan 146–148
P.O. Box 5199
3008 AD Rotterdam

Magazijn *De Vlijt*
Lijnmarkt 48
Utrecht

SWITZERLAND

Fadehax
Inh. Irene Solca
4105 Biel-Benken
Basel

NEW ZEALAND

Peter McLeavey P.O. Box
    69.007
Auckland 8

Sources of information

UNITED KINGDOM

The Lace Guild
The Hollies
53 Audnam
Stourbridge
West Midlands DY8 4AE

The Lacemakers' Circle
49 Wardwick
Derby DE1 1HY

The Lace Society
Linwood
Stratford Road
Oversley
Alcester
War BY9 6PG

The British College of Lace
21 Hillmorton Road
Rugby
War CV22 5DF

The English Lace School
Oak House
Church Stile
Woodbury
Nr Exeter
Devon

United Kingdom Director of
    International Old
    Lacers
S. Hurst
4 Dollius Road
London N3 1RG

Ring of Tatters
Miss B. Netherwood
269 Oregon Way
Chaddesden
Derby DE2 6UR

UNITED STATES

International Old Lacers
Gunvor Jorgensen
    (President)
366 Bradley Avenue
Northvale
NJ 076647

Lace & Crafts magazine
3201 East Lakeshore Drive
Tallahassee
FL 32312–2034

Index